FIGHTING FOR
FREEDOM

Charleston, SC
www.PalmettoPublishing.com

Fighting for Freedom
Copyright © 2023 by Razaw Ghafour

All rights reserved

No portion of this book may be reproduced, stored in a retrieval system, or transmitted in any form by any means–electronic, mechanical, photocopy, recording or other–except for brief quotations in printed reviews, without prior permission of the author.

Hardcover ISBN: 979-8-8229-1572-5
Paperback ISBN: 978-1-64111-670-1
eBook ISBN: 979-8-8229-1573-2

FIGHTING FOR FREEDOM

A Family's Journey from a Homeless Nation

RAZAW GHAFOUR

Table of Contents

Chapter 1 1

Chapter 2 5

Chapter 3 8

Chapter 4 18

Chapter 5 35

Chapter 6 38

Chapter 7 44

Chapter 8 48

Chapter 9 59

Chapter 10 66

Chapter 11 71

Chapter 12 87

Chapter 13 108

Chapter 14 118

Chapter 15 124

Chapter 16 126

Last chapter 133

Chapter 1

The date was March 10, 1996. It was warm and sunny, and it smelled just like spring, which would put a smile on anyone's face. No words can describe the fragrance of that day. The (narcissus) and *Gulalai suwra* (red tulip) were everywhere. The sky was blue; the birds were singing and dancing over the trees. It was just a few days before Nauruz, which kicks off Kurdistan's first day of spring.

My husband, shwan and I were sitting in the front yard of our cozy home in Sulaymaniyah, Iraq. It was about four o'clock in the afternoon, and the house was quiet. My daughter, Lana was playing with her toy doll while my son, Alan was enjoying a longer nap than usual.

My husband and I were talking about how we needed comfortable jobs so we could better support our two children.

Every day, we would spend countless hours searching for jobs. He desperately asked his friends and family for help with any information they may have about employers that were hiring. We both graduated from the same college the same year and had remained good friends through the years.

After our graduation, we grew apart; he went to Baghdad to work at his family business, and I got a job in Sulaymaniyah. After four years he came back from Baghdad to our city. He finally returned and our friendship grew closer. About a year later, in 1989, we got engaged and married.

In 1984, a few months after my college graduation, I started my first job as a library manager. I liked it and gave 100 percent every day, I realized it was not my dream job. I had always wanted to study law and become a lawyer, but sadly, my grades were never good enough. For that reason, I went to study office management at Mosul University (Mosul is another city in northern Iraq).

In 1991, once I had my first child, I requested six months off work to start my new job as a mother. I stayed home with my little girl. I was terrified of taking care of a baby for the first time…I didn't know anything about it.

Although at times it was scary and difficult, I always did my best, and I was very happy. My heart was constantly filled with love and joy for my baby. Having a child opened my eyes to a newer, more exciting kind of love. My heart would beat so fast every time I would see her asleep or smiling! I had never experienced a love like that, and I never knew taking care of a baby could be so exhilarating. I quickly learned how to become a good mother. Being a mother is a wonderful feeling, and I embraced every minute I spent with my child. For me, the experience came with love and time. Six months came and went very quickly, and I had to go back to work.

Although it was time to look for a babysitter, my husband and I wanted to take care of our own child, so I had no choice but to take another six months again to watch after my little girl. I thought long and hard about whether I wanted a babysitter for my little girl, but at the end of the day, it was never an option for me. I couldn't be away from my baby. Taking one more year off work with no pay was better than paying for a babysitter. So, I stayed home for one more year.

It was an exciting choice for me, because after one year, spending every minute with my baby gave me the most wonderful feeling ever. Feeding her, looking at her beautiful, sleepy face, playing with her…those were the most exciting times for me.

We had a lot of fun together! She was very smart. She started to understand me when she was only five months old, and she started talking at nine months. When I looked in her eyes, I knew how much she loved me and wanted me to be with her, but I knew I couldn't always be home with her. One day I would go back to work, but that thought was enough to give me anxiety.

Two years passed quickly. I changed jobs, from a manager to a teacher assistant at the elementary school, just because I wanted to spend more time with my baby. In my country, teachers had three months off in summertime and two weeks in wintertime. So that was how I would get myself more time at home. This happened very quickly, and I started working at school only part time, four hours a day.

I went back to work because our expenses had gone up, and my husband's job was not enough by itself. We had to watch our child together, so we organized the time between us. We both agreed that we didn't need a third person to help us to raise our child. My mom offered to watch her during the week at her house, and on the weekend, we could take her back home. That wasn't a good idea because I couldn't be away from my daughter for all these days and nights. Instead, my mom would watch her for a few hours if we needed her help.

On the day of my daughter's third birthday party, I was delighted to find out I was pregnant again. Nine months later, I had my son, a handsome boy, another angel. Now I had two kids; it meant my life was full of joy and happiness. I'm so grateful for those angels that God gave to me. I pray every day that God helps me to raise them in the best way I can. I love my babies to death; they are my life.

We both wanted to give our kids everything, so we decided to work harder, because now we had more responsibility and two kids.

Once again, I wanted to take care of my second baby myself. it was my pleasure to watch them while they were growing up in front of my eyes, and I wanted to enjoy every minute that I spent with them. They are my world.

Now, my daughter was six years old, and my son was two. I always saw them as the most wonderful, lovable kids. My daughter started first grade at school, and she was doing wonderfully! Her teachers were surprised by how smart she was. This made me very happy. Also, my son was excelling at home, learning to talk very soon and learning to walk even sooner.

I knew they deserved to have a better life. They deserved to grow and be raised in a safe place, a peaceful environment, away from violence and destruction. I knew that once this was provided; my kids would become great people when they grew up.

Chapter 2

The political situation in our country wasn't safe for anybody, except for those who were with the Iraqi government. My husband and I were always concerned about how we could continue to protect our children from Saddam and his regime when they grow up. We would look for ways to leave Kurdistan, either through Turkey or Iran. Of course, this was illegal and extremely risky, and nothing could be guaranteed.

Because Saddam did not allow Kurdish residents to own passports, we had no choice but to stay in Iraq. He didn't let anybody travel anywhere outside of Iraq. He understood that if we left Iraq, we would never come back. We were a nation held captive like birds in a cage. Our hope that Saddam's system would someday take care of the Kurdish people slowly disappeared. The way he treated our people was dreadful, and it grew to be unbearable as time went on.

Every day we heard that groups of people were leaving the country, some going through Turkey, some through Iran—illegally, of course. Even though they knew they might not make it, they still tried. A lot of times, they didn't make it. They got killed because where they were going was very dangerous. The bandit near the border killed them and took everything they had, especially money and valuables. Sometimes they took their kids or women. No one knew what happened to them; they just vanished.

Some groups were deported back to Iraq after being caught by border patrol and were sent to government camps sponsored by the (Baath Party) which usually meant a death sentence for those who tried to flee without permission from Hussein.

Some groups were facing an unexpected situation if they took the wrong route after passing through Turkey, ending up in the jungles and rivers near Greece—especially in bad weather when it was flooding. The people who helped them pass through Turkey took them with a very small boat that could only fit five to ten people, but in order to make more money, they fit twenty and more. They didn't care about what was going to happen after the travelers got off the boat. That was a very dangerous and common practice that was happening to many people leaving Turkey and going to Greece. Some bodies were never found due to many drownings that occurred from overfilling the boat.

The few who made it to Europe were very lucky. They either spent a lot of money or found the right people to guide them. This was an ongoing situation and was headline news almost every day.

Even with all the drama that was happening every day, the travelers still stayed strong and tried to push through the drama. All they could think about was leaving the country as soon as possible. Their positive thoughts always led them to believe that there was a light at the end of the tunnel.

Later, a very small group made it to Europe after many sacrifices, challenges, and spending a lot of money. It was always easier for a single person to pass rather than a whole family. We got used to hearing several horrific stories every day, just like the one my sister told me.

Chapter 3

Chinar was dealing with many problems while she was making her way to Greece with her two kids. Her daughter Tara was four years old, and her son, Twana was barley one year old. Chinar was living with a group of people in Istanbul, composed of two couple, and three single men.

After nine months of struggling in Turkey, they decided to head over to Athens because they been together for the previous nine months.

They worked and watched over each other; they helped and supported each other. They lived in an old house in a faraway area, in the middle of nowhere, which kept that group of people together in the long term. That house looked like it had been abandoned and was in disrepair. Cobwebs were present, and the house comprised seven rooms: four bedrooms, one bathroom, a very small kitchen, and a small family room.

Some of them had been there longer; some of them had arrived just a few months ago. Chinar told me: she had some money when she got to Turkey, just enough for only one month. She wasn't prepared for any surprises or any mistakes. Also, she took some clothes, just enough for one month or so.

Her husband told her, "As soon as you get to Istanbul, call me. I will be there to get you and the kids [he was in Greece already]" He also told her, "I have enough money with me, so don't worry."

Chinar had a nice, safe plan with her husband. As soon she arrived in Turkey, he would be there, too, in one or two weeks at most, and they would all go to Athens together like one happy family. He said, "there would be no fear of Saddam anymore; the kids would go to school and study without fear. They would live in peace with no war, no misery. At least they would be safe".

That was a nice plan. She said, she did as he required, as soon as she arrived in Turkey, she looked for a phone to call her husband (even before she looked for a place), and she called him but didn't get him! She tried calling him again many times that day, but she didn't get an answer. She said, "I was really shocked because he knew what time we would arrive in Turkey, and he told me he would wait for my phone call! Why didn't he answer me then?

"I said to myself, 'Wait a minute, I must call (Mr. No Name) to come and show me the place to stay in, until my husband was coming. Now I must call him!' So, with all my worries and surprises, I called that man. I told him that I was waiting for him. He said, 'he would be there in about ten to fifteen minutes.'

"So that guy, shows up very fast. He was driving an old truck. He said, 'Come on, let's go. We need to hurry up before anyone sees you. Hurry up!' I was still looking at his face. I wasn't sure; should I go with him or not? He said, 'Madam, are you coming, or no? I can't wait on you all day. I'm a busy man; time is wasting.'

"I asked him, 'What is your name?' He said, 'Don't worry about my name. I'm the guy who is supposed to take you to that place that I promised you last week, remember? This is my job, to take care of people like you who are coming from Kurdistan, so hurry up. Don't worry; you must trust me.'

"After I heard that, I didn't let him finish his words. I jumped into his truck. He said, 'You can call me Saeed. I know your name; you don't have to tell me again.' He asked about my kids' names and how old they are. And he said, 'When I get you inside the house, you must give me the money. You know our deal?' I said, 'Yes, Mr. Saeed.' Then he started driving.

"On the way to that house, he told me, 'That house I'm taking you to, it's not like a nice clean house. It's an old, dirty, dusty, smelly, house for people coming for only a week or two, a month or two, just like you, and they leave. They don't care about cleaning; it's just a temporary place, like a rest area. You can call it what you like, but don't worry about anything happening there!' He was talking and talking, telling me about that place. He already made me worried.

"We got to the house after driving about thirty minutes. The house was somewhere far from everywhere. He said, 'You have to be in a place like this, far from eyes; you never know who is watching us. Here, money can make everything possible. People do everything for money.' I didn't want to ask him any questions or what he meant by that. I thought I understood; I just wanted to get inside the house and put my kids in bed—if there was any bed.

"That house looked old and dark from outside, between many trees. You couldn't see it until you got very close to it. I knew why he had chosen this house! More security. So, he stopped the truck, and he told me, 'This is the place. You can only stay one week, because that was our agreement, right?' I wasn't sure that I had to say. He was telling me the truth, but what if I wanted to stay longer? He was waiting for my answer. He looked at my face, and he said, 'We talked about that, didn't we? I know you remember.' I said, 'Yes, yes, we did.' And yes, I remembered.

"And he continued talking about his job and how many more people were waiting for him. He said, 'Please, I have more people coming, so I must be there for them. They can't move or go anywhere. If something bad happened to them, I will be responsible, so hurry and give me my money, for only one week, OK? After one week, your husband comes here, and you leave with him. That was the agreement.' I said, 'Yes but today I called him many times; I couldn't reach him.' He said, 'It's OK He may be busy. I don't know; call him again. Give me money; let me go.' I gave him his money and he left. I stepped inside the living room Chinar continued, "I looked at the room. It was almost empty, there was only one old dirty sofa and one bed on the floor with some pillows and small blanket. There was a small window on one wall—nothing else. I put my son on the bed. He was asleep. My daughter was tired too; she just lay down beside her brother and fell asleep. I looked around the room, it had a bad smell, the walls painted many deferent colors and a lot of memory from previous people was written almost everywhere. I knew other people were living in this house but until this moment I hadn't seen any or heard any! I went to check the hallway. I wanted to check out the house, because he didn't mention who was living there and how many rooms were there. He was rushing to go back to the border.

"While I was checking the house and looking for the bathroom, I heard a man talking and a woman's voice, like they were fighting. They were loud. If I went farther, I could hear more, but I decided to stop right where I was. I wanted to come back to the room where my kids were sleeping, but I had to know who I was living with. I turned to my right. I saw another room; the door was closed, but I saw the light under the door, so I knocked. The man said, 'Who is this?' I said, 'I'm a new guest here.' After one or maybe two minutes, he opened the door. He said, 'How did you come here? We didn't hear anything.' I said, 'Yes, Mr. Saeed brought me here and he just left. My kids are asleep in that room.' I pointed with my finger, and I said, 'I'm sorry I knocked at the door. I just want to know if I can use that room at the end of the hallway, or maybe somebody else is using it?' He said, 'No, madam, go sleep. You are OK. We will talk about it tomorrow. My wife is asleep; you will see her tomorrow.' I said, good night.' He said, 'Good night,' so I turned around and came back to that room. But still I was looking for the bathroom. Finally, I found it; it was in the same room."

Chinar said the next day when they woke up in that room, her daughter asked her, "Where are we, Mom?" It was the first time for them to sleep and wake up somewhere other than their house, so that was something very strange and new for her. My sister said, "while I was changing my son's diaper, somebody knocked on the door."

"I stood up to open the door. I saw one of the ladies who was living in the house. She was a beautiful young lady. She said with a bright smile on her face, 'Good morning. My name is Bihar.' She came closer looked at Tara and Twana she said, 'My God, lovely kids. What are their names?' I smiled and said, 'My name is Chinar. This is my daughter, Tara, and this is my son, Twana.' Bihar said, 'Their names are beautiful too,' with a lovely voice. 'Welcome to our house. Please feel free to ask if you need anything; we all come from different places, but we are here like one family. We care about each other. You're now one of us. Don't worry; We made a nice breakfast, we would love you to share with us.' I said, 'Thank you; just give me a minute to get my kids ready. We will be there soon.'

"At that small kitchen were a small table and five chairs. Each chair looked different, and each chair looked worse than the others. I didn't know how they used those chairs. I wished no one had asked me to sit on any of them, but when I got to the kitchen, the guy I had met last night was sitting on one of them. He stood up very respectfully and asked me to sit down, but I said no, thank you. He said, "Sorry the chairs look bad, but trust me, they are strong." I sat down, my son on my lap, and my daughter on another small chair. He said there were more people living here. They only had five chairs; they never ate any meals together.

"I asked if there are more people I hadn't met yet. He said, 'Yes, we are two couples here, as you see, and there are three more young men. They are living in the biggest room in the house, that room.' He pointed to it; it was at the end of the long, dark hallway. 'They are nice too. You will meet them soon, when they come back today.'

"I asked, 'Where are they?' He said, 'They are working to make money; they are trying to leave soon.'

"The other couple who'd had a fight last night were very quiet, and they looked mad, but they said hello to me and my kids too.

"I had a delicious breakfast with them. The new people just looked fine; every couple had come to this house at a different time. They didn't know much about each other, but they sounded like they knew each other from a long time ago.

That morning I was very worried about my husband, but I couldn't say anything to anyone. I was thinking about Mr. Saeed; maybe he could help me, but he was a very busy man. That day after little chitchat with Bihar and her husband, I asked him if he could take me somewhere to make a phone call to my husband, because I didn't see a phone in the house. He said, 'yes, we don't have a phone. That is for our safety reasons. And yes, I can take you, but it's a long walk. You know we don't have a car; you must walk, and there you have to wait in the line.'

"I said, 'No problem. Let's go.'

"I was holding my son; I wanted to take my kids along with me, but he said, Leave them with my wife. She loves kids; she will take care of them." I wasn't sure if I could do that, but he insisted I leave them with her "The kids can't wait that long in the line. You don't know when you are coming back home. "He spoke.

I said, "OK, now let's go." I was so worried and, in a hurry, to know what happened to my husband. At the same time, I was worried about my kids because I was leaving them with a total stranger, but what could I do? I had to leave them with her.

We got to that place. He looked and asked me if I still wanted to call my husband because of the long line to use one phone. I said yes, I would wait. He said, "But I can't wait for you; it's about two hours' waiting time."

I said, "You can leave, but please, can you come back to take me to the house? "Because I don't know how to get there.

He said, "Yes, but if I come late, don't move. Just wait."

I said, "I will wait. Don't forget me, please."

After a one-and-a-half hour wait, the line was almost done. It was my turn; I was so happy. I was sure when I called him, he would answer the phone, and I was going to tell him that I'd been here since yesterday waiting for him, and when he came here, that he will see his son for the first time. I started dialing his phone number. I called him four times, but there was no answer! I was so angry, so sad, and so disappointed. I stopped for one second and asked myself, what could have happened to him?" A very squeaky voice interrupted my wondering. The lady behind me yelled, 'Hey, woman, let me try. You're just wasting your time. He doesn't want to answer your call.' She was laughing. She pissed me off.

"That day I called him more than ten times, waiting in line repeatedly, until the guy came back to take me back to the house. I was so scared; I knew something was wrong.

"Every day I was doing same thing just to discover any news about him. I asked Mr. Saeed if he'd heard anything about my husband; he always said, 'no. I didn't hear anything.' A day before one week had passed, Mr. Saeed told me I could stay until my husband showed up, or until I heard anything from him.

"As much I was sad and worried, I was happy and excited he let me stay. I tried hard every day to convince myself that maybe my husband was sick, or he had an accident, or maybe he was helping people from Athens to Europe. But my heart told me that something bad happened to him.

"I knew he was living with three guys; they were working and living on the same farm somewhere close to Athens. They were helping an old, wealthy couple. That wealthy man was a generous person. He let them stay in a small apartment he had on that farm just to help them to save their money. I knew my husband was working hard to make money for us, to transfer us to Athens and later to Europe. He was making good money. As he told me, he had left Kurdistan one year earlier because he wanted to make it easier for us and to find a better way for us to leave. At that time, I had only my daughter, but I had been nine months pregnant with my son.

"I tried to call his friends; I didn't find them either. I got to the point that I thought he was not alive. Something bad had happened to him. There were other ways he could have answered me, or at least, one of his friends could. It was just pointless.

"Now what could I do with him not answering me? I didn't know what to do by myself with two kids. Ah, God, tell me what to do! That was the first disappointment.

"I tried calling him every day. I had to walk one hour and thirty minutes to find a phone and then wait about one hour in line until my turn, but I never got a response. I kept asking here and there about him. I didn't get any answer; it was just like he had vanished. My life started getting more difficult. The money I had was almost gone. I had no idea where my husband was. I was thinking about going back to Kurdistan, but everyone told me no; if I went back to Kurdistan, I would never find my husband, but if I left Turkey, I would be able to look for him more. I believed it was very possible I had more chances to find out what happened to him, so I stayed in that house. Then I had to find a job, just like those people, to support my kids and myself.

"My job was cooking and cleaning the house when everyone left for work, and when they came home, I had to go to my work. My job was only for a few hours. but sometimes I had to stay longer. I helped a nice lady at her grocery store, but my kids stayed at home with Bihar. She watched them until I came back home. I worked every afternoon until late at night, but every time before I finished my work, she told me to take anything I wanted for my kids; she wanted to help me. she didn't know much about my life,

I believe good people are everywhere; wherever we go, we still find good human beings.

"I worked with her for quite a long time, but I couldn't save enough money for my trip to Athens, Greece. Every time I looked at my kids, I felt sorry for them. I held my kids, kissed them, talked to them. I told them they were all the family I had; they were my life and my love. My daughter always asked me, 'When is my daddy coming here to take us? When we will be together again?' Every time she asked me those questions, I looked for the right answer to tell her, but I never found it. I didn't know the answer. Maybe we would never get together!

"Six months passed. We were still in the same house. We were getting to know each other better and trusting each other more; we had just become one big family. They adored my kids; everyone helped with them. My daughter, Tara, called them aunt and uncle. She loved them like her family. I thought I was blessed because I was surrounded by good people like them. They did a lot for me and my kids; they were always watching over us.

"We started talking about when we should leave Turkey. We had to save and to find a trustworthy person on whom we could depend on to make our trip easy. We all agreed on the date to leave.

Chapter 4

"Mr. Saeed decided to send me and the whole group with his best friend, Mr. Murad, to Athens. This guy was supposed to be a very knowledgeable person about the routes and know the safe way to drive or even walk to get to Athens. Mr. Saeed said he would have liked to take us, but unfortunately, he couldn't do it that time. I took a lot of food and water for us and extra clothes. I was lucky enough to have good people with me for that mystery trip, so the money I saved from my work, I gave to Mr. Murad.

"Everybody was ready and worried, especially me because of the kids. It was after midnight. The kids were already tired and sleepy. We had been waiting for Mr. Murad, more than one hour. After we became more panicked, he showed up with his ugly old truck to take us close to the Greek border, but of course on a different path that not everyone would use. The truck was like a small bus with no seats. He put some blankets and some pillows in to make room for us. We had to leave sneakily. It was cold, the middle of January. We left at that time because of our safety; we had to hide ourselves from the Turkish border guards.

"After we got far enough from the Turkish border, we found ourselves among a group of thieves, a lot of them with dangerous types of weapons. They stopped us. First, they asked for our money and our clothes and then our food. They were very savage; they took everything from us.

"They didn't even let me have my kids' food. When I was begging them to let me have my kids' food, they told me, "These kids, they will die anyway! So, you don't need food or anything for them." "They took almost everything from everyone: money, clothes, and food! After those thieves took everything, we had. We weren't sure that we had to do. We were scared to go back; I wasn't sure what would happen if we went back; everyone had a different opinion".

"We finally decided to walk. It was very cold; we had to walk at night and sleep during the day. I also had to keep the kids quiet, so I gave my son a sleeping pill to make him sleep all day and night. While we were walking, I was holding my son on my back, but my daughter was walking. Everyone helped me to carry Tara because she could not keep up the pace with the group. After walking two days, I knew my kids, especially my son, Twana, were not doing well. He started crying a lot. I tried very hard to keep him quiet because we shouldn't make any noise. If someone around the area heard us, they could call the border security on us, and then we would be in big trouble. I was very concerned about my kids first, and those good people with me second. They start getting scared because of my son; he could cause problems for other people. I know they will not say anything to me, but I saw they walked very fast. It was like they wanted to leave me. I knew why, but in my heart, I felt so sad, and I didn't want to say, "Please don't leave me here alone." I couldn't blame them. I knew what would happen if we got caught. Everyone wanted to survive.

"I could not walk fast as fast as they; I was getting slower and slower, but they were almost far away from me—about a half mile. Bihar came back. She said, 'Hurry up; we can't make it if you are slow like this,' and she grabbed my son from me. She said, 'Oh my God, he is very hot.' She continued talking, telling me, 'They are not waiting for you; you better hurry.'

I was having back pain already because I was carrying my son and sometimes my daughter, too, with one small bag. It wasn't heavy because the thief took most of stuff I had for my kids.

After we had been walking together about thirty minutes, we were silent. I was thinking about what would happen if they left me behind. Suddenly she gave me my son back, with a few box of cookies. She said, 'I hide this from the thief for your kids. Please forgive us. We are sorry, but we must hurry. Please take care of yourself and the kids. I promise if we get to any place close by, we will send you help. Just take this road; don't make a right or left, just go straight, OK?' it's only one and a half day left.

"I said OK with my voice cracking as I tried to choke back my tears. I said, 'Thank you for helping.' I know they decided to leave me because I was very slow walking. So, after fifteen minutes, they disappeared from my eyes; I couldn't see them anymore. The sun was rising; it was almost another new day, but I knew this day would be the most difficult day for me.

"I didn't give up looking for any place to hide from dangerous animals or people, so I found an old, destroyed house. I went inside to rest my feet, legs and my back. They all hurt so bad. I knew my group was already gone, so it was only me and my kids.

I had to be strong enough to survive; I had to face everything by myself.

That place was very old; it had a very bad smell. It looked like a big house from a long time ago, but the whole house had been destroyed for some reason, except one room. It was in better shape compared to the rest of the house. It had only one empty room of furniture, but it was full of dirty clothes and just garbage, nothing good. Plus, it looked very creepy. After looking for anything I could use to make a fire to keep us warm, I did find something. I found humanoid bones, covered with dirt, and shoes that looked very old. After I saw that mess, I became terrified, but I didn't have any choice. I was very exhausted of walking and carrying my kids. I put my kids on the floor, but I was still looking for any piece of material or wood—anything to throw our tired bodies on.

"After inspecting every corner, and going throw dirty piece that laid here and there, everywhere, inside that room, finally I found something that looked like a big tent. I pulled with all my power, but it was very heavy because, of the dirt was stacked on from many years. I made a small fire with the wood and pieces of junk from that room. At the same time, I had to be careful to not make a big fire, to avoid attracting attention. If someone unintentionally saw us or sneaky people found us, we would be in big trouble. So, after three days, we finally had a chance to sit down and get some rest. I gave my kids the cookies from Bihar. I only gave them two pieces. I had to keep them alive. I didn't know how many more days and nights we would be out. I touched my son's forehead. He was extremely hot. He had a fever, but the good thing was that the thief left their medicine for me. With all the sore I was dealing with, I felt so happy because I had my kids' medicine.

"I gave my son the medicine. Soon afterward, my kids both fell asleep. We stayed there in that mystery house until the next day. That night was the longest night ever for me. I was praying to be alive until the next day, and I would leave soon. That night I heard voices. I saw people all around that house talking, but I couldn't understand anything. Their talk was not clear. They looked like shadows. They were fast. Some looked young, some very old. They looked busy. Their voices were loud sometimes. Sometimes I heard some whispers. The whole time, I closed my eyes and pretended that I was asleep. The room was bright, but I knew it was dark outside. I knew it was night. I was sure I was awake and not dreaming.

"That time I figured out why the whole house had been destroyed except that room the house was haunted! When the sun rose, the room was quiet. I could only hear my kids breathe, but the room was very cold. We were almost frozen. I opened my eyes. I didn't see anything, just my kids with the ashes from last night's fire. I started to make a small fire again and would leave as soon as I could later that day.

"We remained in that cold, dark, scary jungle alone. After walking one more day, I didn't see anybody coming to help us or anyone around. Before the sun rose, I started walking again with two sick, hungry kids. After two days of walking alone, I saw a small river from a long distance. I ran toward it to drink water, thinking maybe we could find something to eat in it. I used my hand to give water to the kids; then I started drinking and drinking with no hesitation about whether the water was clean. We were thirsty; all these days past, we had been walking without drinking, so after we got enough water, I started looking for something to eat. I found a small frog. I wasn't sure if I could catch it, but because the poor frog was frozen and couldn't move, I caught it easily. Then I had to look for something sharp to cut the frog. It was a disgusting idea, but we had to eat at least my kids did. We were very weak.

I never imagined in my life that something like this would happen to me. I cut the frog to pieces with a sharp rock that was there and gave it to the kids to eat. Spuriously and willingly, the kids ate bloody, raw frog because they were hungry. They wanted more. They would eat anything, I believe. Unfortunately, it was the only live frog in that frozen river. After the first wild meal, we started walking again. I was thinking about how many more days we could walk without food and water. Maybe we would not find another river or another frog to eat. Maybe that thief had been right when he told me, "Your kids are not going to survive." In that moment I felt my heart tear apart for my kids. I closed my eyes for a minute. I wished that we would all stay alive and survive together, or that we would die together.

"I was almost barefoot because; my boots were worn out, so I couldn't walk any farther the way I wanted. It was difficult walking with my boots. It was almost useless. It made me sad and upset, but I had to keep going. We took a break every thirty minutes because; I was holding my son on my back, and my little girl was walking, but when she slowed down, I had to hold her too. It is impossible to describe or explain what we were going through.

"That situation become more difficult with every minute that passed. I was very tired, cold, and depressed—complicated feelings. I had to think about how we could get through this to its end. One minute I was positive that we could make it because I believe in God, and I know God never disappoints me. God always helped me. The next minute, I thought this was our end. I blamed myself. I felt awful for my kids!

"The bad weather was extremely against our hope and our goal. Our journey got more and more difficult. We were tired, sleepy, and hungry again. We had nothing to eat. The only food we had was snow; there were not even any leaves.

I was looking for any big tree or rock or anything we could sit beside. I was looking for any type of shelter to protect my kids and myself from dangerous people or animals until the next day. I didn't know which type of animal may live there, especially in the winter. I thought they were hungry too; they were looking for food, so we had to keep going. Suddenly my daughter looked around and asked me, 'Mom, did you hear that?'

I said, no, 'what did you hear?'

She said, 'I don't know. Hold me, Mom, I'm so scared.' She couldn't describe what the voice was like, so I said to myself, 'Maybe she said that because she is tired and wants me to hold her.'

A few minutes later, I heard the wolf's howl. What? They were wolves. Yes, I was sure! Even though they weren't very close, it sounded very scary. I asked my daughter if that what she heard. She said, 'Yes, Mom.' And she asked me what it was.

I said, 'Baby, don't worry. We will be OK. Don't be afraid!' But in that minute, I became more horrified than ever and panicked. We still walking, but I tried to walk faster.

"It was dark. I couldn't see anything anymore around me; it was just quiet and scary, so I decided to take a rest. During the last couple of hours. I was thinking about going back, but we had been walking almost five days. The road was covered by snow. We ate some snow when we were thirsty, but there was no food. We finished all cookies we had, and not even one frog. I think the frog we ate was the only one alive.

"I was too tired to walk more than ten minutes of every thirty. I was losing all the energy I had but if I went back, I would have had to walk ten more days. And by that time, the kids would die. There was no chance to survive if we went back, but if I kept going, maybe someone would come to rescue us. I was very confused about everything: the hunger, cold, not sleeping for many days. It made me not think well sometimes. I was very negative and disappointed, but sometimes I thought positively that God was with us and would help us. I didn't want this happen, not for us, not for our kids. But I must live for them. I was really scared when I saw my son start coughing very badly. He was barely breathing. He had a fever. I was praying the whole time.

When it became dark, we heard a lot of wolves. Sometimes I feel them very close to us. It was extremely scary, especially when I was alone with two kids and didn't have any kind of weapon with me to defend of myself, and my kids. I was thinking about how hard we tried to live our lives normally, just normally, with no pain and no breaking hearts. Why couldn't we have that life in our country? I didn't think it was too much to ask. I wish that everybody, everywhere, can live in peace, no war anymore, no pain, no blood. Kids can sleep in peace. We won't be worried about ourselves, our families, our kids. Now we had a lot to be worried about. Our past was all about hurt, kill. And now it's my present. I was living in a big painful mystery. I was afraid our upcoming life would become a bigger stinging. With all my bad thoughts, I still had hope, and I felt something was pushing me to keep walking and not stop. I always remember that after rain, there is sunshine (and I never believed it because in our country, it's always raining). We hadn't seen that sunshine yet. Maybe one day.

"With all my thoughts and crying, I just stopped thinking for a minute. I said to myself, 'Hold on; did I hear something? Somebody calling me. Or maybe I'm hallucinating!' I asked my daughter if she heard anything. She said, 'Yes, Mom, I heard somebody.' We both heard somebody. The voice was coming closer and was getting clearer. When I looked up, I saw the man. He was still about twenty-five meters away from us. I saw a short, fat man calling me, asking what I was doing in a most dangerous area alone with kids.! first I didn't say anything; I just stood up. I was shocked. I couldn't say anything; I didn't know if what I saw was real! Then I ran to him. I asked him, 'Who are you? Are you looking for us? We are lost. Can you take us with you please? Don't leave us. My son is very sick.'

"My little girl called him. She said, 'Please, we are hungry. Don't leave us here alone.' We were running to him and talking, asking him questions. But he said, 'Stay there; don't move. Don't go anywhere. I will be back. I will bring my truck to pick you up. Just hang in there.' When I heard that, I just fell on the ground, and I looked up to the sky I said, 'God, please make him come back for us, if he is real.' I was crying. I didn't know why talking was difficult. I couldn't move my lips to talk that time. When my hot tears fell over my cheeks, I knew my face was frozen. We didn't believe what we heard! Was it real, or was it a dream? I asked my daughter if we had seen a man. She said, 'Yes, Mom, he was wearing a hat.'

'Did we talk to somebody?' I asked her.

She said, 'Yes, Mom, he said he will be back.'

'Did you see him?'

She said, 'Yes, Mom, I told you I saw him.'

"I wasn't sure. I was very weary. We had been walking for almost six days. We didn't see anybody, and suddenly this guy came here alone and didn't take us with him! He left us. What was he doing? Why didn't we see anybody else with him? So many questions came to my mind. But if he was real, how could I trust him? Who knew who he was? Maybe he wanted my kids! Again, bad thoughts were coming back to me. I said to myself, 'It's too late to make any decisions, and now he knows a woman with two kids is desperate to get out of this dark, cold, scary place. But if he comes back with his truck, I will go with him; maybe he is a good man. If we stay here, we will die here anyway. So, there's no chance to survive here."

One more time, I must think positive. *God, help us*. I asked God to send this man back to help us. "I said to myself, 'I must be more patient and wait. He will be back. He looks real because he said, 'I will bring my truck,' and he said, 'Don't move.'" He had repeated to us, "Remain here; don't move." Then he just disappeared. Maybe he is close to the road.

We sat back and waited on him about twenty minutes. We were very cold, and very panicked. I didn't know what was taking him so long. Did he want to come back and help us? I asked myself if something had happened to him. Should I go? Or wait? He didn't say how long I had to wait! And now it was getting dark. If we stayed longer, we would be frozen. It was sunny that day; we felt a little warm, but when the sun started to set, it was very cold. And sometimes it was a little snowy, but not all day. That day was warmer than the past days we had been through.

"We waited on him more than forty-five minutes. He didn't come back. I gave up waiting. I decided to go. Sitting in one place was not good; in a situation like that, you must move, not wait.

I started walking again for about thirty minutes. I was very tired and hungry. My kids started crying again, asking for food. My daughter couldn't walk anymore. She was very weak, and my son couldn't stop crying too. I try to keep him quiet, but he was very sick. I had given him all the medicine I had.

I looked for a tree or anything to sit under to hide me and my kids. I found a big tree. There were no leaves because it was January. I didn't see anything but mud, so we couldn't walk anymore. We sat once more. We were miserable. I held them both very tightly to my chest. I tried to keep them warm. My son's fever was very high, and my daughter started coughing, too, very badly. She was asking me when we were going home, are we going to live like this forever? Could we have a house anymore? I couldn't answer her; I just wanted her to be quiet because I wasn't sure about anything. In that minute it was like a mystery. Would we survive, or would we be animal's food? We were a target for anything, human beings, animals, bad weather, sickness, hunger, anything. Anything could kill us. However, I tried so hard to keep my kids and myself alive.

"I told my daughter, 'Baby, let's think about tomorrow when we wake up; everything is going to be different.' I told her to just pray, to ask God to help us and keep us safe. She started praying until she fell asleep. I tried to keep my hopes up and to be more hopeful about how we could do it, no matter what, but I saw that my kids were going down every minute past. My son's health got worse. I said to myself, 'This is our end; we will die tonight.'

"That night I prayed. I talked to God. I said, 'If it's our end, please forgive me if I made a mistake for bringing my kids to this endless nightmare. I'm so sorry; I'm just a mother who wants a safe place for her kids, and I want to find a better life for them. I didn't want them to be killed by Saddam. God, I'm a powerless, weak mother right now. I need your kindness; I need your help. I'm an incompetent mother. I don't know what to do; you are the only one who can help us. Nobody knows where we are but you. Please, please help us; we are so scared."

(My husband was wanted by the government in Baghdad because he had been working in a sleeping cell with Peshmerga. My family was absolutely in danger in my country. We were not allowed to be in Kurdistan). That night I prayed and ask for forgiveness.

I was crying so hard and very loudly, talking to my God, when I felt a big hand pull up my son from my lap. Somebody said, 'Sh.. sh…, it's me, Saeed.' I jumped from my place. I just grabbed my son back, and I said, 'Don't touch my son, please don't.' I said that without looking at his face, and I asked him, 'Who are you?' He said, 'Saeed.' I told you I'm Saeed.

"It was getting dark. I couldn't see him clearly, but he whispered in my ear. He said, 'Shhhhh, please don't be afraid. I'm so sorry that it took me longer than I expected. I'm back to help you and your kids.'

I said, 'Who are you?' with a sharp voice He said, 'my God women! I told you. Please just follow us. You have to trust me. I have come back for you and the kids. Come with us and hurry. I'm here to help.' I thought it was only Saeed, but there was another man who held my daughter and walked away very fast. I said, 'Wait, I don't know this man.' Saeed said, 'Please, we don't have time. We should hurry. Walk as quickly as you can.' They didn't know how miserable I was, but I just followed them.

I didn't know the other guy. I didn't trust him, but I had no choice. What could I do if I did not go with them? Did I have another choice? Of course not. Because of the dark, I couldn't see any of their faces, and they were walking fast. I tried to go faster, but I couldn't because my boot was torn. I had almost bare feet. I was the most miserable person in the world.

After walking a couple of minutes, Saeed looked at me and said, 'Take this blanket. Put it around your shoulders. It's cold in here.' I said, 'No, put it on my kids.' He said, 'Don't worry; we have brought some for them too.' And they already had put blankets around my kids.

Then I knew they had come to rescue us. But why had they left the first time, when they knew I needed their help? Even though they knew I had two kids with me and that we were hungry and cold! but now they came back? I said to myself, 'Now they are here helping us?'

In that minute I looked up, and I closed my eyes. I said, 'Thank you, God.'

I saw that the man looked at my son's face, suddenly he asked me in soft and worry voice if he was alive. I said, 'Yes, of course. Why do you say that?' I took my son from him very quickly. My son was very hot. I said, 'Why did you ask me this question?'

He said, 'Nothing, it was just a question. He wasn't breathing normally.'

I said, 'How long do we have to walk? You said the truck is close? Where is your truck?'

He said, 'Very close. Please don't worry. He will be OK.'

My heart was beating hard. I was expecting that my son wouldn't survive that night. He said, 'Please just hurry. We don't have much time.'

'My daughter can't walk. Please can you hold her again?' His friend said, 'I will take care of her.' I couldn't walk faster like them because my boots were torn. I had tied them with a piece of my cloth. I was pushing myself to reach them.

"We walked about ten minutes. I saw a big truck was waiting for us. Saeed said, 'I told you we were close. See, this is the truck waiting for you and your kids. Jump, go, hurry.' I jumped inside the truck. I was so happy but so worried about my kids.

"There were about ten more men and women there, inside the truck. But they looked much better than me and my kids. Everyone tried to help us to get inside the truck, and they are looking at us, surprised that we were still alive, especially my kids. We were in very bad shape and were very clumsy. No one could believe we were still breathing. Everyone looked worried about us, and everyone was asking if we were OK. They were asking, 'How are the kids? Are they OK?' I wasn't sure. I didn't know. They were not. Those people knew we were out in that jungle, just the three of us for almost six days.

My group had gotten to Athens. They told Saeed that we had been left behind on the way to Athens in that jungle. So, he decided somehow to come back looking for us with his truck with the other new group. They said they had been looking for us, but they couldn't find me because I went the wrong way. Saeed told me all this later.

Everyone inside that truck was asking me different questions, like how we had gotten that far. Even I didn't know how. Maybe because I walked at the nighttime when was dark, and I was looking for food. There was that time I thought I had lost my direction, but the only answer I had was only God. God wanted us to be alive; That was my only answer about how we survived.

"They give us food and water—just a little. One of the ladies had a little boy with her. She asked me if I wanted an extra jacket for my daughter because my daughter was shivering of cold, even though she had a blanket on her. I knew she was sick too. I didn't let her finish her question; I said, 'Yes please.' She took my daughter very nicely and asked her, 'What is your name, beautiful girl?' She wasn't sure if she could answer this question. She looked at me to ask if it was OK to tell her name, because a few days ago, I told her, 'Do not talk or answer any questions if strangers ask you anything until I tell you it's OK.'

"The lady didn't ask again, but she put my daughter close to her chest and said, "Poor girl, she has a fever." And she gave her more water to drink and took off her blanket, and she said, 'We need to hurry up.' She looked at the other people. She said, 'We need to tell him the kids need a doctor. Their health is getting down.'

In a sad, angry tone of voice, I told her my kids they were not going to make it, because I heard them say, 'We still have ten more hours.' She asked me how my son was. I said, He doesn't respond to me.' I was looking at him; he was very pale; I was crying. She was holding my daughter. She came closer to me. She said, 'Give me your son; let me see.' I said, 'No. If he dies, I want him to die on my lap.'

She said, 'Maybe I can help you. Please give him to me.' I was very sad and panicked. I didn't want to; she had a beautiful-looking face. She looked like she had a good heart.

She was just the right one for us in that very tough time. I gave my son to her. She gave me back my daughter. She looked at me and said, 'I know how you feel. Please try to calm down and relax. I'll try to do my best.' And she held him on her lap. She asked the man sitting beside her to give her his flashlight. Then she looked at my son's face, and she took everything off him. When she took off his socks and his gloves, she looked at me and said, 'Did you ever check his fingers or his toes?'

I said, 'No, why?' She said, 'Nothing, it's OK. He will be OK. Don't worry; I just want to ask.' Her voice had changed. She looked worried, and she asked the same man to give her a backpack with a first-aid box. He gave to her; it was in the corner with the other stuff they piled up. It was dark inside the truck and outside as well. I think the time was 6:00 p.m., but to me the time was the same. I didn't feel the difference; day was like night. All my attention was on my kids and praying for them. I didn't want anything except for my kids to do well and to be healthy. If somebody had asked me to give my life away for them, I would have said, 'Yes, please take me instead of them.'

That lady was checking my son's body very carefully. She opened her bag and took out something from the first-aid box. She looked at me. She said, 'Don't look.' I said, 'Why, what you are doing?' She said, "Please, I want you to trust me. I'm a nurse; I can help your child. I know what is wrong with him. Let me do what I can do for him. If you want him to be alive, it's all up to you. But he is not doing good!" I wasn't surprised, but I couldn't say anything; all I was doing was crying. She said, "tell me yes. We have nine more hours to get to the nearest hospital, maybe more. Who knows?"

Another lady had been quiet the whole time. I hadn't paid attention to her or anybody else who was there until they said something. As I said, it was very dark; I barely could see their faces. In the beginning she looked like she didn't care about anything just herself, she was with her husband and seemed very quiet and careless about what was going on, but finally she starts saying something. She said, "Let her do it. She is very good; she can help your son. We all trusted her all this time we've been together, so let her do her job. He will be OK. Your son almost died; at least let her try." She said, "Oh, by the way, my name is Cheman, and this is my husband, Kareem." She looked very young; maybe she was only twenty years old, maybe a little older, but she looked smart. She said, "But we don't know what your name is?" I totally ignored her; my mind was with my son, and with this nurse and what she could do for my son.

Her voice was very sharp; it cut the silence. She yelled at me. She said, "Now, what do you want to do? Don't you see him? Do you?" I said, "I do, but I'm so scared. Thank you for caring, but—"

She interrupted me and looked at the nurse and said to her, "Nazanin, don't listen to her, just do it!"

I didn't say a word, but she understood why I couldn't make any decisions, so she didn't wait one more second. She quickly gave him a shot and put a small needle all over his toes and some of his fingers—they all had turned blue because of the cold.

Later she also gave a shot to my daughter, Tara, and they both fell asleep. Anyway, they all helped me very much. The truck did not stop, not even one time, until we arrived in Athens after six days of walking and ten hours of driving.

Chapter 5

That was my sister's experience. Millions of other Kurds faced the same fate as they tried to leave the country to escape Saddam Hussein's regime (the Baath party) and their atrocities. This was the reality for most Kurds who attempted to flee the country through the Turkish border. Many young Kurdish boys and girls drowned in the Black and Aegean Seas, and many more lost their way in the snowstorms and were never found. Most who were found were found frozen.

My sister was reunited with her husband upon her arrival to Greece. She discovered through Saeed that he had been imprisoned for working on the farm with his friends without legal papers. Saeed knew about this the whole time. He hid this information from my sister to keep her head clear while she fought to get herself and her children to safety. She sent me a letter soon after her arrival, explaining what she could about her situation. She could not tell me everything, she said, because what she experienced was impossible to fathom. She warned in the letter, "Do not risk your or your children's lives trying to leave the country through Turkey, or any other border, illegally." She wrote, "Sometimes it's impossible to put your feelings on paper. What I went through with my children was beyond any reality I could have imagined. We cheated death by a miracle."

She was begging me not to think about leaving the country until we found a legal way to do so. Her words and her experiences were largely the reasons I wanted to continue to stay in Kurdistan. My sister is very strong and has a brave heart. I'm always proud of her. She was and is the perfect example of the bravery of Kurdish women.

My sister and her family settled in Europe. After one year, she gave birth to her third child, a beautiful baby boy. They have settled in well despite their traumatic past. Her daughter is currently studying for her master's degree in science. Her oldest son is in his second year of college studying biology, and her youngest boy just graduated high school.

Most of the time, when the family, or even a single person, got thrown out of Turkey, if they were not successful, the Turkish *jandrma* (Turkish border control) arrested them. If they didn't kill them, they would send them back to our country. Saddam would then execute them gladly.

That was a big risk for us too. I didn't want to put my children in a situation like my sister's. What happened to my sister is beyond reality. It was a miracle, and miracles don't happen every day. It was another reason that my husband and I were still in disagreement about leaving the country. We both had big families who cared for and loved us. They would be worried if we left the country. We would be worried about them, too, perhaps even more than they worried about us. I loved my parents. They were very kind, considerate people and were not young anymore. My brothers and sisters where are all there, with the same hope that they would someday leave Kurdistan. They were all married with children too. I loved them all, and when I thought about leaving them, it gave me severe anxiety, especially after the daily horror stories we were hearing about other refugees. It was a saddening feeling to live among your family and friends in your own country, yet to fear for your life in what is supposed to be your home. When you do look for a way to get out, how and where you want to go becomes insignificant. The goal is only safety and survival.

My brothers and sisters were also searching for an opportunity to leave Kurdistan, without hesitation. Although my husband and I were both searching for this opportunity, I hesitated to believe that I was ready to take this step and risk our family's lives. How could I possibly leave my homeland and family behind, and continue to hold onto the hope of ever seeing them again? I cannot express in words the depth of my love for my parents, siblings, and their children. I was more accepting of leaving my place of birth than I was about leaving the people who made that place a home. I could feel my heart tearing to pieces as the time to make this difficult decision approached. So many distant family members, dear friends, and neighbors fled the country every day, making it impossible to withdraw from the thoughts of leaving. I tried to remind myself that although I loved my family, the safety of my own children was the priority. All I knew was that I would be willing to sacrifice everything before I allowed Saddam Hussein to hurt my children. No Kurd felt safe in this country if Saddam is alive.

Chapter 6

Each day's people sold everything they had houses, cars, furniture, anything they owned to buy their own lives, from him (Saddam) and his system.

I remember as a student in college they would regularly come to classes and randomly took students. No one knew why. No one could ask any questions. The only thing you could do was just follow them, because that was the only way you could save yourself from a bad beating in front of the class. Those horrible incidents happened almost every day, at any college or high school or middle school. At the dorm many times, even the teachers were not allowed to ask where or why you took him or her, because most of the time, they knew the answer. A lot of the time, we never heard anything from those kids anymore; they just disappeared. That made students terrified. Soon, if they got any chance to run, they would leave the country. We used to be very careful what we were doing at school or at college. We had to be very careful about whom we were talking to, what we were talking about, and with whom we were hanging out.

Everything was questionable from the government. We had to be careful how many times we were going back to our city to visit our family, and for how long we were staying, and with whom.

What they did to us, as teenagers was abuse. Mental abuse. They wanted us to be constantly thinking about them and afraid of them. They wanted us to not trust our best friends, or our neighbors, or even our family. They tried to break us down. They tried to make us weak and cowardly. But they didn't know that was making us stronger, angrier, and thirstier to fight for our freedom. After all, what they were practicing with students, generation after generation, was not helping the system at all. The result was more upset than what they want to see.

Unbelievably, they were attempting more and more to abuse us (college students), to get us to sign their agreement paper, a contract between the government and the other party. If you signed, you must give them (the government) any information about anything you know, with all details. They didn't care how small the information was, but they needed to know everything, with a lot of explanation. You must let them know any simple movement about anybody, your neighbor, friend, or anybody you don't know. Basically, they wanted you spy on your people.

They put you in one position. If you helped them, you stayed alive, but if you didn't cooperate, they would fiend away to hurt you until you tell them anything you know. They wanted to know if anyone related to the Peshmerga, because every day people joined them, and sometimes a lot of families sent them help, like food, clothes, shoes, medicine, and so forth. They fought for us.

That little help was nothing compared to what they did for us. We wanted to show them how much we appreciated their service.

Saddam always tried to start with young people or, I should say, a new generation. He was trying to brainwash them, to make a battle inside our Kurdish community, to be a big help for his future. It didn't matter if they were students or not; he knew that young people are much easier to scared and threaten; and poor people that needed money for their families. Everybody wanted to live and have enough food for their kids, so he was always looking for those types of people. Those kids, they needed to have a future and finish their college to live their lives. Or if they had businesses, they needed his permission, so everything seemed nearly impossible to do in my country. He believed that if you were not with him, you were against him, so he would make a bad case for you or anyone. It would be easy for them to come to your house and take you from your family, who would never see you again, most of the time. If you were lucky, or if your family had money, they could find somebody to help find you. You were very lucky if you are still alive after they beat or hanged you for one week, or ironed all your skin, or had their savage dog's bit all over your body; that happened with my uncle. Saddam's men took him from his office because he was a lawyer. He defended innocent people. He was just starting his job. He hadn't yet completed his first year. One day he didn't come home. After three months of looking for him, we knew that he was at a jail south of Baghdad (Abu Ghraib). It was one of the very bad, special jails, most created to torture Kurds. If anybody went there, it was almost impossible for them to be survive more than a few days. They judged people without any questions asked or any trail made.

My uncle and thirteen more lawyers, engineers, and some doctors were arrested. Form Saddam's special force, they put them into that jail, without any investigation, just because they were new graduated, they just start their job. They had a lot of motivation to do their job, in addition, help poor people. Some of them didn't even been in a politician side or helping any line that against Saddam's system; they had just started their jobs, but Saddam always had to do his part first.

After nine months of enduring mental and physical torture, some of them unfortunately were assassinated. Some of them were executed, but my uncle was the lucky one. He came home after one year. I can say the first time I saw him; he didn't look like himself anymore. He was miserable for a while. They had been torturing him many hours, every day for nine months. They tried everything with him, but he didn't admit anything he had done. He didn't tell them how he was helping sleeping cells inside the city; he didn't tell them how my grandfather helped Peshmerga. He was sending food and clothes to them, plus he was sending money to their family.

The only time they let the people out of their jail after a few days was on one condition: when they signed the agreement, that person agreed to give them any information about anyone, even their brother, but if they did not agree after all, they would be shot, and their body sent back to their families. And their family must send money for the bullets they used to kill their kids! Sometimes the people singed the agreement just to save their lives, and when they got out, they ran away to connect with Peshmerga, or they left the country like most Kurds did. In that case, Saddam's system got his or her family instead. No matter what we did, no matter how we acted, we were not safe inside our country. He treated kids like adults, rich like poor, men like women, educated like uneducated. Everybody was a criminal to the Baath system because we were all Kurds. They just wanted to be more ignorant. So, at that time, you must think about everything very carefully before you made any movement. That was how we were spending our lifetimes.

Every day passed in our life with a new, sad story. But we always had hope that one day, it would be better. If we were together, we would make it better. We never stopped fighting for our independence.

Our Peshmerga, or "those who face death, the Peshmerga," along with their security subsidiaries, were responsible for the security of the regions in Iraqi Kurdistan. Peshmerga always defended Kurdistan. They fought for our independence. They never gave up. They sacrificed every value they had for Kurdistan, for Kurdish dignity. For us they sacrificed their lives, their families. For our land, language, our freedom, our rights, our civilization, and for our history. Saddam and his regime wanted to take everything from us not just our souls, but our land, everything we owned. This was just a drop in the bucket compared to what he has done to our people.

I want to stop talking about our ugly, painful memories that are buried inside our hearts; we never forget our pain because we lost a lot of our sons, daughters, people we loved, people we know, and friends with whom we grow up.

All this violence, sadness, darkness, and discrimination become very big parts of our daily lives. Our reality was hard to forget. It was our wrecked childhoods, our terrified teenage years. It was hard to forget our friends who sadly disappeared without knowing why or what was done to them.

It was hard to forget our family members who were killed most of the times for no reason. We never forgot those bodies; they used all different ways to torture them to death and then sent them back to their parents. How could we forget our young girls and boys, whom they been raped and tortured to death?

I don't want to talk about that time anymore because I believe if I want to talk about everything in detail, I will need at least one thousand pages, and it still would not be enough. So, I'd better stop right here, and start talking about my family and our journey to the United States.

Chapter 7

I'd like to talk about my story and tell the whole world about how my family and other Kurdish families came to the United States. The way we came to the United States was one of the hardest and was difficult time for us. Coming to the United States was a big dream for many people. The people who wanted to leave Kurdistan couldn't think about the United States because of many reasons; We know that America is a very big country; it's very far away from Kurdistan, and it's out of reach. But at the same time, it's full of freedom in many ways, which every Kurd thirsts for. We want it.

I was dreaming that my kids would grow up there with all the advanced technology and higher education. My dad admired the American lifestyle. He loved to watch American moves. He also liked to read a lot of American novels. His favorite movie was *Gone with the Wind*. He also read the book of the same drama many times, until one day I asked him why he loved this book. He said, "It's an American love story; it's an interesting story."

He gave it to me to read, but I said, "I wish, but you know my Arabic language is not good enough to understand." That book was translated into Arabic. I hadn't learned Arabic yet, but it was in my mind that one day I would read that book too. I did and I really enjoyed it.

We also admired the United States for many reasons, like the freedom and the right to vote, freedom about language, religion, ethnicity, speech, travel, education, work, and much more. We knew if we went to America, no matter where we go, we would feel safe. We would be able live our lives much better than in Kurdistan.

While we were in our own country, we couldn't sleep in our own beds! We hid from Saddam's weapons when he was bombing our city when he was at war with Iran. We couldn't study in our own language (Kurdish). We weren't allowed to learn or read our Kurdish history books. They took it all away or destroyed it, but they couldn't take the soul of our history; our history is living inside us. Thousands of years ago, our forefathers made that history, and we continue to make this history every day. They tried to erase our leaders' names, like Salah Aden Alaube, and our heroes, like Qazi Muhammad, and many, many more of our brave countrymen.

They also burned the map of Kurdistan and many books that showed the real Kurdistan borders from four sides—north, south, east, and west—just to confuse the young Kurdish generation from knowing their true history. They tried to hide any acknowledgment from us about our race and our truth. Being a Kurd was being a criminal to Saddam's regime. We couldn't go to visit our relatives if they lived in Baghdad or farther south unless they asked hundreds of questions. They always made us feel like we were living on the land where we are strangers, like it wasn't our country for many, many years. Thus, going to America was a big dream to almost everyone. But it was also very difficult.

Kurdish people went past many borders to get to Europe and save their lives years ago. But no one was planning or even thinking about going to America, except a very few people who went back in the 1970s. They started their lives, beginning with going to college. They had very successful lives; they became doctors, lawyers, writers, and so forth.

For us, going to the United States wasn't an option. It wasn't our choice; we never, ever planned to go to the United States. Now I can answer the question, *why?* Even going to college wasn't our choice. It was his choice; he didn't let us have many options. As a kid I always worried about my dad because of the dictator Saddam, because my dad had his own business. He was a professional. In his job, he worked with exports and imports of different types of material, from the only country that Saddam had traded with. My dad was in that business more than fifty years, and was very honest, honorable, and truthful. He was a practical and successful man, responsible for his business and his family. He never cheated in his job. Anything that was bought or sold was legal in his store. My dad worked seriously for many years; he made good money. But the problem was, nobody was left behind. Saddam had something special for everyone, even the decent businessmen like my dad and many others. Saddam, as usual, always had something for Iraqi people, especially the Kurds—this time something beyond the imagination of anyone. He asked for a very generous donation of gold from all businessmen like my father! Yes, a lot of gold. If they could not afford the required donation, they would lose their businesses! We all know he meant what he said, he was always serious. And he would also take away all the money they made. Who knew what else he would do. Of course, we know the rest!

The reason for collecting gold was because of the economic blockade our country was going through at that time. He wanted to make a very big statue for himself from the solid gold. If the gold was not enough, they had to give him money to finish his statue. Day by day, our fear grew. Now that we were grown up and had a family and kids, our lives become very risky. Saddam made everybody wish to run and leave their own country. He made our lives very miserable, with every day worse than the day before. No one could make any decisions about anything. We thought and thought, but we didn't know how to make the best choice. That was life in our country and how we dealt with the dictator every day for a long time.

Chapter 8

My kids were very young, and I didn't have work. My husband had lost his business. He was working between Sulaymaniyah, my city, where we belonged, and Baghdad, the capital of Iraq. His job was to export and import food and other items for his small store. Sometimes he had to stay in Baghdad one or two days, or sometimes he needed to stay more to get his stuff and bring it back to our city.

Going to Baghdad and coming back to our city every other week wasn't a good idea. But at that time, working with government in the office was not for everyone. I considered myself lucky when I started working in the office three months after my graduation. But many people didn't get a job, even if we all graduated in the same year. After graduation, the young Kurdish people split into three groups. The first group looked for a job. If they found the right job, they accepted. Sometimes that job wasn't their dream job, but they had to accept. Then later, they dealt with whatever was happening to them. This group was just a few, not many. Just like me, a second group did not agree with the conditions, or they didn't find the right jobs they wanted because of their political circumstances. After they got tired of being jobless, some wanted to start families, so they stayed with their parents. And they had to accept their lives; however, some never got jobs, so Saddam called them for the military and then sent them to war.

If they didn't connect with military, he would find ways to arrest them and then kill them. Things like that were very easy for Saddam to do. So, this group experienced risk and left the country in very difficult circumstances and difficult situations. Some got to Europe successfully; some didn't get anywhere unfortunately and were killed, lost, or deported back to the country.

The third group stayed and tried to work with a family business maybe survive maybe not.

When Saddam become nastier and more discriminating with Kurds, the Peshmerga become stronger than ever, not just in their faith or their belief but also in their numbers. My husband's job was from the third group. He worked with a family, to support us me and my kids. It was a risky job any time he left the city. He had to go through many checkpoints. After ten minutes of driving, he would go through another checkpoint every five to ten kilometers. It was about security guys checking everyone's ID passes. They were looking for anything to make people become angry. But we learned to play their game, not giving them any excuses. Most people learned how to be patient and did not show them how they were destructive, murderers, corrupt people. Everyone was tired of them; however, sometimes, young people couldn't take their bullies and persecutors, and they were taken and were never seen again. My husband's job made him go through all this at least once every month. Any time he left from home until he came back, I was expecting that anything could happen to him. Maybe we would never see him again; it was very possible. He was making good money. We always had extra money, but he had to take a dangerous path. So, I had a very bad time whenever he left until he came back home. I didn't want my kids to grow up without their father. Many times, when he was going to Baghdad, I didn't expect him to come back. I thought, *I'm going to lose him one day*, and when I was thinking about that, even only for a minute, I felt like my life would end with that. So, I asked him to look for a different job, something better and safer, inside the city.

We started searching for a job. He was jobless almost one year. I was working, but not at a regular full-time job because of my kids, so the money we saved from his job was almost gone. We decided that we would not think about leaving the country soon until we could find a legal way and the kids grew up a little more. At least my son would be able to walk.

Time was passing day by day. We keep searching, asking friends, people we know, about a job; but nothing. Our lives were getting difficult. It wasn't acceptable, especially when you had kids. You must have a job; you must do anything for them to keep them alive and happy.

On January 25, 1996, we heard that an American organization was on its way to Kurdistan to help the Kurdish people. It was a big surprise for everyone. Every day, this news became more real, and the news of this new organization coming in to help Kurdish development spread like wildfire.

In the beginning, no one believed that news; it was only between people, not on the television news. Kurds' reactions were very different. Some people were happy, some were scared, and some were angry. None of them understood why America was coming to help the Kurds now. It was good for many reasons and not good for others. People didn't believe they were coming to help us because that was too good to be true. People would ask out of suspicion, "Did they not realize how much we needed their aid at the time of Anfal? Were they not aware of what the regime was doing to our people? Why would they come to our aid now? What are their intentions, really?" We desperately needed US intervention a long time ago, and we didn't get it. Therefore, among all these suspicions, some also believed that the only intention of the US was to provide military aid to Saddam or reopen negotiations for oil trade. Despite our suspicions, we were hopeful that the US organization would arrive with the intention of helping the Kurdish people to safely thrive in their homeland. Our people's mistrust was justified, simply because so many of our people had witnessed their children being raped and murdered by the regime—everything you can imagine, for many years and years. Saddam used all his power; he used all his weapon to kill Kurds. He tested new weapons over Kurds. The whole world knew about it, but nothing happened from them. No one stood up for the Kurds. We fought Saddam; our Peshmerga, our heroes, defended us. Where was America?

    He still was taking any advantage if he had any chance to get revenge on the Kurds. In 1991 we had taken our independence from Baghdad's regime. He was always threatening Kurdistan that he would be back one day, and his revenge would be very hard this time. He said he was still thirsty for Kurdish blood. Again, the American organization was a big surprise, because if they came to help Kurds, where was America? When Saddam used chemical weapons at Halabja in 1987 and killed ten thousand Kurds, my best friend was one of them. She had just started working in a small elementary school as a teacher. Her family never found her body. Somebody said she was burned with a chemical gas when Saddam attacked Halabja. Many innocent women, kids, and men were killed in only thirty minutes. And we know America knew but didn't do anything against Saddam. After that Saddam destroyed about four thousand villages, big and small, from 1987 to 1989.

In August of 2019, a ThoughtCo. article titled "Crimes of Saddam Hussein" was published by journalist Jennifer Rosenberg, detailing the attacks against the Kurds:[1]

Hundreds of thousands of Kurds fled the area, yet it is estimated that up to 182,000 were killed during the Anfal campaign. Many people consider the Anfal campaign an attempt at genocide. As early as April 1987, the Iraqis used chemical weapons to remove Kurds from their villages in northern Iraq during the Anfal campaign. It is estimated that chemical weapons were used on approximately forty Kurdish villages, with the largest of these attacks occurring on March 16, 1988, against the Kurdish town of Halabja.

---

[1] [His] regime carried out the *Anfal* (Arabic for "spoils") campaign against the large Kurdish population in northern Iraq. The purpose of the campaign was to reassert Iraqi control over the area; however, the real goal was to eliminate the Kurdish people permanently. The campaign consisted of eight stages of assault, where up to two hundred thousand Iraqi troops attacked the area, rounded up civilians, and razed villages. Once rounded up, the civilians were divided into two groups: men from ages of about thirteen to seventy, and women, children, and elderly men. The men were then shot and buried in mass graves. The women, children, and elderly were taken to relocation camps, where conditions were deplorable. In a few areas, especially areas that put up even a little resistance, everyone was killed.

Beginning in the morning on March 16, 1988, and continuing all night, the Iraqis rained down volley after volley of bombs filled with a deadly mixture of mustard gas and nerve agents on Halabja. Immediate effects of the chemicals included blindness, vomiting, blisters, convulsions, and asphyxiation.

Approximately five thousand women, men, and children died within days of the attacks. Long-term effects included permanent blindness, cancer, and birth defects.

Where was America? No one wanted to help; The Kurdish people were disappointed. We didn't believe anybody. We did not believe that there was any power above his power (Saddam's) because he had money to buy every kind of weapon; Unfortunately, he did. That is why we only believed in our Peshmerga, the only real, pure spirit that could fight against Saddam, they bravely, truthfully, honestly fought for our rights, our democracy, our dignity, our freedom. Kurds become all one power in North Iraq in 1991. We killed all the ignorant people in our city who were worked for Saddam. They got what they deserved, one after another. Everyone went out to fight, young and old, men and women, even kids. Peshmerga came to the city the night before, and we were ready for just one signal to start, and we did. We cleaned our Kurdistan from those savages, from those bloodsuckers who had been living on our people.

We kicked them out. After several bloody days and nights, we got our independence from that dictator, that savage, who was living in Baghdad (Saddam). We had a bad past and not a good present. because We were still dealing with enemies inside our city, of course unfortunately always there is a type of people who will do anything for money. We still had some of them; it wasn't a big group, but they were large enough to hurt people.

We knew Saddam still had a hand inside our Kurdistan, cheap people helping him to do whatever he wanted to do. Saddam bought those dead-hearted people; he paid them good money if they gave any information about anyone. he was very generous with those people.

A few months later, we heard that an American organization already done a lot of great project in Kurdistan and they had done a very important job.

Decent things happened from these organizations. They started building a simple complex and small villages for the people who lost their houses after they were destroyed by Saddam's bomb. They also built hospitals and schools. They tried to hire people as much as they could, men and women, young and old. They didn't care who you are; they just tried to help people to give them opportunities, to have a job, to make money, because many people were unemployed for many years, just like my husband. We heard from a friend that they were looking for the people who could speak English, who able to travel, and who could stay more hours at work.

In the beginning, the first few months, they didn't require a lot of qualifications, but after a few months, they started to ask for more experience and qualifications, so hiring a new employee wasn't that easy anymore. They hired every type of engineer to build houses, hospitals, and roads. And then they looked for people who could speak English and who graduated from college with a bachelor's degree or associate degree. After that, they wanted a lot of monetary workers, drivers, cooks—basically they hired for every type of job.

There wasn't only an American organization; British and Sweden organizations also came to help our country. They did almost the same thing in Kurdistan. Some of them brought medicine, some brought food, and some of them fixed the roads inside and outside our city.

They did big favors to Kurdistan, which make the Kurdish people love them and appreciate what they were doing. Kurds started trusting them; they became our very close friends. They understood Kurds, they started communicating with Kurds, they made good friends with us, and they knew how our lives were with that dictator. It's very different when someone tells you the story and when you live in that story and see things with your own eyes. I know Americans heard a lot about our past, and present, and they heard what Saddam did to Kurds. But they couldn't help us at that time; probably they had their own reasons, but when they came to Kurdistan and they heard a lot of stories from real people, also they saw much evidence. They saw the realty of our live. In that time, the American people understood our life, they shared our tragedy, and they felt sorry for us. That time, they were sure that we had been under that dictator's power for all those years past. Now we wanted to leave our lives safely and peacefully. We wished to make the best lives possible for our kids; we wanted our kids to grow up in a clean environment.

On March 14, 1996, My husband applied for this job through his friend, and two days later, they called him for an interview. He didn't believe how fast they responded to his application; it was fast. They told him he need to be there before 8:00 a.m. He was ready one hour earlier. He was awake all night. He couldn't sleep; he kept asking me, "What do you think? What questions will they ask me? Do you think they will hire me?"

"Maybe they will, why not? You graduated a college, you can speak English language, and you like to work, not just hard worker but smart worker too. so, I don't think they had a reason to not hire you," I said to him. That night he was worried about everything.

The next morning, he was ready to go to his interview. He was dressed nicely and shaved very well. Then we had a happy breakfast together. The kids were happy, too, even though they didn't know what was going on. Then he said to me, "Please pray and wish me good luck." I prayed for us. I told him, "Honey, they will accept you. I'm very positive." He smiled and kissed the kids; then he left.

After they asked him a few questions, they gave him a test on his English language skills. He passed the test, and then he got the job the same day. My husband couldn't wait to come home to tell me he got the job. He called me soon he got the job he was so happy he said, "I got the job, and I'm starting tomorrow." I was even happier, that day quickly I get ready I went to my parents' house to tell them. They were happy for us too. He started working on March 24, 1996, my son's second birthday.

On his first day, my husband didn't look happy; instead, he looked worried. He took a shower and shaved, as usual, and again dressed nicely. He didn't know what exactly his job was. I asked him why he didn't look happy. He said, "Because I don't know if this job is good or bad! I don't know what is behind it; maybe it's a good opportunity for us, or maybe we're opening a door of hell for ourselves." He wasn't sure about his job yet or what he would be doing, we were still not sure about Saddam's reaction about America's project in Kurdistan.

We had some freedom in our city, but Saddam was still alive. He still had domination over some areas; he had a lot of special forces too. The first day at his new job with the Global

Development Center(GDC) organization, my husband wasn't very happy; I knew something bothering him, but he didn't want to talk about it.

He was right. I knew why he was scared. And look worried! I understood what he was thinking about. We had been living all these years in trepidation, fear, and injustice, I didn't want him to start his first day like that, I asked him if he is not happy then he shouldn't start this job at all, because we both knew "This is a big problem and very serious. We know how much Saddam hates Americans and Kurds. Now we are both working together! So that means he hates us twofold. What if one day they left the country? Then, we'd be in big trouble. I know no one will support us!" he said, "We need this job. And we don't know yet; maybe I should try.

If anything happens, we are not alone. Besides that, we can't live like this forever. Either you or I must have a serious job to raise our kids. There are many of men and women like us. They've gotten jobs and worked with them."

He felt a little better and put his shoes on. He kissed the kids and said, "Wish me luck," and he left.

I was a little worried, too, but I had a good feeling about it. I was excited—maybe because it was something new. We didn't have any experience with working with anyone from the United States! I didn't know. Maybe that day I had a strange feeling. It was a long day for me because I was waiting for him to come home and tell me how was his first day at work, and what is his job title? what is his job like? What was he doing with Americans? I was happy and worried I had many questions to ask him. But he came home after 11 hours, he looked happy and not worried! It was about 7:00 p.m. That was a long day for the first day of work.

He told me there were many good people working there too. He knew some of them. He said his job wasn't hard, but they would send him to another location. It was a one-hour drive from our house. We were happy.

A few weeks later, we start inviting my husband's friend from work to our house for dinner, and slowly we almost got to know everyone he worked with. We had a very good time with his new friends, and their families too, because we all had kids almost the same age. We did many birthday parties; my husband was a very generous man with me and with everybody. Later he started buying new furniture, and anything the kids and I wanted. He always wanted to make us happy.

After a few months, my husband proved himself as a sincere, earnest worker, so the supervisor gave him more work to do, and more locations to monitor and supervise of course with an increase in wages. His supervisor gave him a raise, and sometimes he gave him extra money because of his loyalty and honesty. Day by day, he spent more hours at work, and he loved his job. I was very grateful. Our lives got better. We were happy; we didn't lack for anything. Our life had become much easier and more convenient. We wanted to rejoice; we wanted to forget our painful past and begin a new, happy life together, so we tried to have fun as much we could because we didn't know what the future held for us. We always saw surprises from Saddam's system, from near or far.

Chapter 9

We had a nice small house at a nice area, not far from my parents' house and a small car. It was enough for our family. We had very nice furniture; my family and friends who came to our cozy house didn't want to leave; they liked our home. Our house had two bedrooms—a nice size—with a kitchen and a big living room, a family room. We had a basement for extra stuff, and upstairs were two extra rooms. It was enough for a couple of family members to stay over. I miss that house. Whenever I think about my house, I cry. I had very good memories there, especially when my family all came over and when we cooked, talked and laughed. especially when we had a birthday party or a religious holiday or a New Year's party, we all gathered in my house. Our kids are almost the same age as my sisters' and brothers' kids. My daughter is older by three weeks than my nephew; my son is younger than my niece by five months, so the kids are all friends and cousins too. We really enjoyed our time with my family and my husband's family. My house was very cute. Everybody enjoyed themselves and had a good time there. When I delivered both my kids, my family and my husband's family stayed over in my house for seven days. It was a most beautiful time. Our lives were starting to be normal and fun.

My husband worked every day from 7:00 a.m. until 7:00 p.m. He was happy about his new job. I was happier because my kids had more fun. At least his job was inside my city, Sulaymaniyah. I wasn't worried any longer about him. I knew what time he left and when he was coming home. Everything was calm, and we were just starting to think that if we both worked like that, we could buy a new car soon. We had many plans for the kids. The time was going very fast.

We always had something to worry about, but things always changed in my country. We always waited for surprises, no matter how happy we had been. Still, we felt we must be prepared for bad things to happen at any minute.

Time passed by and everything was calm for a few months—until one day in September of 1996, when my husband went to work, just like any normal day. After he left, I fed the kids. I gave them a shower. Then I started to clean up the kids' room and our room, as usual. The kids' toys were everywhere. Later that day I got the kids and myself ready to go to my parents' house. We used to gather every Thursday of the week and sleep over to the next day, Friday, with the rest of my sisters and brothers. I was almost ready to leave, but I heard the kitchen door open. We usually used the kitchen door when we are going out and coming home. But when I was home alone, I locked the door from inside, so that was something not expected. When I saw my husband already inside the kitchen, it wasn't expected. It was too early for him to come home—at 11:00 p.m.—unless something had happened!

My daughter ran to him to hug him. She was so happy that her daddy was home! She said, "Mommy, my daddy's home." I look at him. He looked away. He was trying to avoid me to not asking him why he came home early. because since he starts working there, he didn't take one day off. Also, when he left, he was ok he wasn't complaining about been sick or anything. Plus, He loved his job. He wanted to be at work every day.

I went into the kitchen to ask him if he is feeling sick? Why was he home? When I looked at him, I saw him with a very grumpy, worried face. He was quiet, like he was thinking about something, or he didn't believe what had happened. I ended his silence by asking him, "Why you are home? Did you forget something?"

He looked at me and said, "Nothing, I just don't feel good. I wanted to come home. Or am I not allowed?"

With an angry voice, I said, "Why are you angry? Of course, you are allowed; it's your house." In that minute, I knew he was hiding something from me.

I asked him again, "Really, are you not feeling well? What is it you are complaining about? Do you have a headache? Is that why you're home? Or maybe you trying to hide something from me?" I was asking him questions one by one. I said, "You know I'm strong enough. I can handle anything. Just tell me what happened at work."

He tried to not look at me, he wasn't answer me at all he ignored me the whole time, then he calls Alan our son he holds him. He was looking around the room. Like he lost something he was putting Alan very close to his chest like he wanted some comfort, that showed me he was hiding a big problem. I said, honey listen to me "No matter what happened, we are a family. We must be together and face things together. If you don't tell me now, you will tell me later. Please tell me now I can't see you like that" He knew I was right. Sooner or later, he had to tell me, but he was still in shock. He didn't know how to say it.

My kids were very happy to go to their grandparents' house, but they felt something was not right. They knew Daddy was not happy. They both tried to reach their father with their small hands. My daughter was trying to hug her daddy. She said, "Daddy, what is the problem? Do you want to go with us?" She tried to make him forget what had happened at work, because she was so happy to go to her grandparents' home. She thought if he went with us, that would help him feel better. My son started cringing because he saw his daddy wasn't happy.

My husband was standing in the kitchen. He looked like he was still thinking about it. He pulled out one of the dining chairs and sat down, and put Alan, on his lap. He looked at me and said, "Do you know what happened last night?"

I said, "No, I don't. What happened? Tell me, please." I sat down on another chair, beside of him I was waiting him to tell me what happened. He said, "I really don't know what to say! I'm very surprised." With a shaking voice.

I said, "About what?" why you surprised?"

He said, "all of American, British, and Sweden organizations left last night without any clue."

Where did they go? Why did they leave? I was just shocked with my eyes open wide, and my mouth open wider. He was talking, telling me the details. I was listening, but I couldn't talk back to him because I was still thinking about the first sentences when he said they had all left us behind. He continued, telling me how he found out that all the groups left. He said, "When I got to work this morning, I saw our stuff. The employee in the front of the office door, where our manager and supervisor are working. He said, 'We have been waiting for our manager or his assistant about one hour. No one showed up.' We asked each other what happened. What is going on? Where were they? Are they OK? We really got worried about them. They had always been at work before everyone else. It had never happened before. If one of them was sick, what happened to the rest? Why did they not come to work? We decided to wait one more hour, but that was too long to wait for someone to come to work. I thought maybe they had a meeting somewhere. But then we got really panicked after we started calling them, but no one answered. "So, they had tried to wait one more hour, and then they had tried to call their home again and again, but still there was no answer.

He said, "They tried to call another US organization that was working in Kurdistan. Someone responded to their call and said, 'We don't know what happened.' They left too! Everybody at work is just surprised, and now we don't know what exactly happened, and where are they? Are they still in Kurdistan somewhere? Or did they go back to the United States?" This was in September 1996.

I was still listening to him, and he was continuing to talk, but my mind went elsewhere. I started thinking about what would happen to us next, thinking about what made them leave. I'm sure they had a good reason. He called me. "Are you listening to me?" He was still talking. He said, "Until now we don't know much about what happened, but I'm assuming that Saddam has something bad for them, and for us as well, but I hope I'm wrong."

We both stopped talking. We were thinking about what we would do next. We always knew nothing stayed nice forever especially in our country, as long Saddam was alive.

He looked at me sadly and said, "now we are facing a big problem. Only God knows what the reason was and what will happen to us!"

What happened that day was one of the worst days in our family history. That day it was a big, radical change in our life, from top to bottom. I knew each change is a turning page. It is about closing one page and opening another one. Changes bring new beginnings and excitement to life, but we didn't know how that change would affect our life. It would be for a better life or worse. You grow and learn new things every time something changes. You discover new insights about different aspects of your life. You learn lessons even from changes that did not lead you to where you wanted to be. Even if you resist or avoid it, it will enter your life just the same. When you initiate the change yourself, it's easy to adapt to it because it's a wanted one.

The thing is, if you live in this world, you are subjected to the same chaos, the ups and downs, the good and bad, the positives and the negatives of life. What sets you apart from others, though, is how you choose to deal with the situation. I tried to think positively. Maybe what happened was for our benefit. But some bad voice was always in the back of my mind, telling me things were getting bad, but I tried to show myself that I was not worried, and it was happening for a good reason—at least in front my husband. I was wondering why we had to experience this while knowing that it wasn't just our family going through this.

That day we were supposed to go to my parents' house and gather with my sisters and brothers, but I called my mom and told her about what had happened. First, she was so surprised just like us. Then, she tried comforting me, saying that who knew what was happening. Maybe this was a good thing for us. My mom was saying that God always has a better plan for us, but we had to be patient.

Chapter 10

That night my husband's friends from work came to our house. Everybody was worried and scared. They were coming and going, talking and listening. They looked very helpless after that strange event. Everyone had different news, different thoughts, and many questions. But we didn't have one answer; we were just like them: clueless. We tried to listen to the news, but there was nothing there. So, we had to be ready for one big change. I know that each change is a turning page. It is about closing one chapter and opening another one. Changes bring new beginnings and excitement to life. I keep repeating this to myself, But I didn't know what that change would be.

"They couldn't wait until the next day to tell us why they have to leave?" my husband was asking himself, "And what they do about us? Those living us like that? we had many questions to ask, but no one could answer." we both started wondering how our life would be. We are thinking about what steps we should take. We both agreed that what happened has something about the Baath regime in Baghdad. We both knew if we didn't hear from the Americans, that meant we would be in big trouble with Saddam. We hoped we were wrong. I remember when I said to my husband, "We are still afraid of him, even though we have our democracy, but because we know him, he doesn't let Kurds stay in peace, he always wants to fight with Kurds."

His friends stayed until late that night. What was waiting for us? Why couldn't us Kurds dream about our future? Why couldn't we plan anything, not even for the short term? Why? And many others wondered why.

We went to bed, but neither of us could sleep. The kids were sleeping, and we hadn't told them anything yet. I'm sure my daughter would have understood if I explained to her, but my son still was not understanding what was going on, so we kept that to ourselves.

The next day we woke up with someone knocking at the door. My husband opened the door; it was one of his very close friends (Jalal) who looks very worried. After he sat down and we had breakfast, I asked him, "what had made him to visit us that early morning" He never had done that before. It was 7:00 a.m. He said, "I don't know. Everybody is talking about you guys." (He meant people who worked with Americans.)

I asked, "Like what?" He said, "Are you serious? You guys don't know what happened?" We both said yes and no! "Now you are here. Tell us what you know; maybe you heard something."

He looked at me and he said, "Yes, this morning I heard something. I hope it's not true, but since you guys don't know, maybe I should tell you then. It's not good news." We both were really giving him all our attention and waiting him with impatiently. I think when he saw us looking very worried, he said, "But maybe people just make it up. I'm sorry to be the one who tell you that, but yes, it's not good news." He tried to hide how much he was looking worried too.

I said, "Please, we have been thinking about everything since yesterday. Whatever it is, tell us now. We need to know." I was trying to hide my fear and worry. I said, "We are not alone; it's about more than a hundred of people." But my husband was quiet the whole time, not saying one word.

Our friend (Jalal) finally said, "Two days ago I heard that Saddam's troops are ready to attack Kurdistan, and control the north again, with all their big tanks and heavy weapons. Of course, American people will be attacked, too, because they are helping Kurdistan now, and the people like you guys are the most targeted. So, when the news announced in *Al Thawra* [the most significant Iraqi newspaper], as soon as the American organization knew this news, they ran away. Without hesitation, they left Kurdistan."

When he was done telling us this horrible news, we didn't say anything. We kept looking at each other. It was one of the most difficult times in our lives. We knew something was about to happen, but we didn't expect it so quickly. Now it was happening, and we had to act very fast. That was what we were afraid of.

Everyone started to become more panicked, and disappointed. We thought they came here to help us, and now they left. Who knows where they are? Where they went? It was a very scary moment. We knew something extremely bad was happening, but we didn't know how to act. What should we do? Which step should we take? Where would we go? My heart was beating fast. My husband and I kept looking at each other for a while without saying anything. We were both shocked. I couldn't think about anything at that moment, but we had to find a way. Then we started thinking and talking about what we could possibly do to keep our family safe. After many hours of talking back and forth, his friend left, and we remained at home. We wanted to find a way for our family to be safe together, but we both had difficulty thinking right, because neither of us knew how much of the news was real.

Later that day, my parents showed up. I was so happy when I saw them coming to our house, because they usually didn't come unless we invited them. I knew they had heard about the news. I said to my dad, "Why are you guys coming for a visit today? It is such a surprise! Do you know what happened?"

He said, "Yes we do, that is why we are here." They looked very worried. My dad said, "We came to tell you, you should leave your house and come with us. Staying here is dangerous for all of you." My dad was very serious about going to his house. He said, "Because they might start looking for you and anyone else working with the Americans. Now they left, and you have no one to defend you. Only God knows what Saddam has already planned to do with all of you." My dad was saying that, and his voice was shaking. I knew how much he was worried about us. He said, "I don't want any resisting. Just hurry up. Pack your kids' stuff and leave this house. Come along with us. Don't tell your neighbor or anyone where you are going."

My mom said the same thing over and over: "Your dad's right. Hurry up before anybody comes. Don't trust anyone these days. People do anything for money." She was right. We knew that.

My husband said, "No, we will stay in our house until we hear if he really sends troops to the city. Maybe he just wants to scare the American group to send them back home to America. Maybe it's just a trick." I really wanted to leave with my parents, but when my husband said that I thought maybe he is right, so I stayed at home.

That day was very stressful. We didn't know if it was the truth or just one of Saddam's games. I was wondering if we stayed home, what would happen? Maybe this time, they would come and take my husband, me, and my kids, and everything would become true. He will kill them in front of my eyes, just as he planned. Or what if we left, and everything was a lie? But I didn't believe that Saddam would do nothing to the Kurds, especially after all the American groups went back home. He always took any chance to destroy Kurds; now he had a perfect time to do anything he wanted. He still considered himself as the head of Iraq, and he was still the only leader in Iraq, north to south, especially Kurds.

Chapter 11

After a few days we know the truth about the news. The news said, "Americans must leave the country in only twenty-four hours. We will execute all the people who worked with those American organizations." Saddam believed that anyone who worked with Americans were traitors. They deserved to be executed—the news was clear on that statement. But some people denied that. They said it was another of Saddam's tricks, just to terrify people, or to make the Americans leave. But what if he meant it? Now who wanted to risk his family's life?

That day everybody was talking differently, giving us ideas about what we should do, where we should go. And we had to hide, at least disappear from people's eyes, even if we only did for a few months. But my parents' idea was the best.

We are in a bad situation, and we must leave. But how could we leave after we settled down? And we decided to stay in Kurdistan, to work hard to raise our kids and build a great family. That was our plan for our family.

My husband was worried more than ever. It was a very critical time. We didn't know if we should go or not. We didn't take the news as serious as in the newspaper. But what if its serious? We couldn't gamble with our kids' lives. Then our plan must change. I knew that the Kurdish situation was always bad, with the government in Baghdad. But for a little while, he was calm with Kurdistan after fighting with Peshmerga, and we earned some independence in 1991. But we always know he was waiting for the right time to take his revenge on the Kurds. His announcement was clear! And as we knew, Saddam disagreed with what they were doing in our country. They were helping Kurds, and we were helping them. So, to Saddam, we were both his enemy. And he believed they were not building or developing anything in Kurdistan or anywhere else in Iraq. But they were looking for something else, like chemical weapons. And now Kurds were working with them; we were both working against Saddam. Besides, the first big, hated enemy of Saddam is America. We all knew that, but they came to help us. We loved to work together; we Kurds believed that "my enemy's enemy is my friend." so now. He has a big excuse to execute us. The people working with these groups were about six or seven hundred or maybe more. I'm not sure about the numbers. People from many different organizations were hired. They adopted a lot of families. They gave a chance to a lot of people who had lost their jobs. It was a big help for Kurdistan to rebuild again and help people to work and feed their kids. They built a lot of construction in and around the city; they built hospitals and schools. They built many housing complexes. They were very serious about helping Kurds. They were very happy about what they had done for us.

Soon they become our friends. People trusted them and were happy to work together to rebuild our country again, even in a better shape. They only felt safe with Kurds and trusted Kurds. They ate our food, they visited our families, they celebrated our holidays with us, they learned about our culture, they experienced our lives—the past and present, how difficult it was. They suffered for the Kurds. They understood our lives. We knew a little about the American people. We treated Americans for the first time in our country in the best way we could. After a few weeks of working with Kurdish people, they knew Kurds, they knew our culture. We respected people who respect us. We were honest with our friends. We were loyal to those who supported us. We made our guests feel safe. If it cost our lives, we never forgot the favor.

So, we heard day by day that the news was real. After what Saddam announced in the newspaper the president of USA Mr. Bell Clinton, announced a very different news about all American employee and their family in Kurdistan. that we will take all our Kurdish employee to America, as soon as possible. after this (good news) for most of the Kurdish people, we felt relief. but it wasn't something we wanted to do at least in that time, but it was making the government in Baghdad to calm down for a little while and wait to see if we Kurd leaving the country or not? Because he was happy about the American government determination, so he gave us three months to sell everything we had and leave the country. Soon we knew that we had only three month we start to look for a realter to buy our house and someone to buy our car, and then our furniture—basically anything and everything we owned. It had to be sold soon. The only thing we were happy about was that we had time to do all the selling

Everything we owned—it was like a piece of my heart. I loved it all so much. We worked hard to earn anything we had. It was very valuable, at least to us. We had been in that house since we had married, almost eight years. We had started a family in that house. It meant a lot to us. That house was our loyal, secret friend who knew everything about our family drama and the very good times with our family and friends. Now I had to leave all this behind and go?

My husband and I had a short love story that ended with a marriage. All our first love secret, it started with that small car he had, when he was coming to my workplace for no reason, just to give me a ride. every day I was using a bus to go to work and coming back home after work to my parents' house. We both named the car Cutie. When he told me how much he was in love with me and how much he wanted me—the only one that knew about us was small Cutie.

Now we had to give our best friend away (the car); we had to either sell it if we found a good customer or just give it away. It was difficult to give up everything we had: the house, the car, the furniture. I called them our best friends, but it wasn't just that; it was our life. Basically, we had to give up our life, because we had to leave our home and go somewhere, we never imagined. It was very, very different.

No one knew how hard it was to give up your life forever, and we didn't have a clue where we were going or what would happen to us.

Whoever reads this story, put yourself in my place. Can you imagine how you would react to an event like this? If it's happened to you, to leave all your life behind, everything and anything belonging to you—what do you do? This included very personal things that we were not allowed to take with us, just our memory, and money, if we had it.

When we first started building a family, we both worked hard to buy most of our needs. Our family and our friends also helped us to meet the rest of our needs. Our house in the very beginning looked like a twenty-year-old's house. We both were very talented and creative; we both built and designed that house. We were happy about our life together, with our family, our friends, our neighbors—and now we had to give up that life forever.

The time was very difficult. Now we had to look for someone who wanted to buy the lovely pieces of our nest at a very cheap price. I felt like my heart was tearing apart. They were all valuable, expensive in my eyes. I'm not talking about their prices; I'm talking about something more than that. I try to explain more about those days that are still in my mind, those days I'll never forget. Those days were momentous days in my life. It was my first journey.

At the same time, we decided to put everything up for sale, seven hundred more families were selling their stuff, too, everything they owned, just like us, in the small city, so finding someone to buy our furniture, car, house, and other items was not easy. Again, it was a tough time.

I'd thrown a few conventional yard sales before and decided that I didn't have enough time to wait for people to swing by and root through my things. Instead, I used one main platform to sell items, bringing that buyer home to check out our good stuff and give me the right price for our items. A few buyers came that day. Everyone was looking at the stuff, surprisingly, because we just started buying new furniture just a month before the American organization left the country, so almost everything was brand new. They felt bad but they didn't give us much money.

We needed to act quickly because we didn't have enough time, so my husband found someone to buy our stuff. He was my brother-in-law's friend. He came one afternoon, and he looked around the house. He looked at the kitchen, living room, our bedroom, my kids' bedroom, my family room, our guest room, our China cabinets. I had three of them with a lot of expensive China sets and a lot of silverware, a lot of nice plates, a lot of antiques, and many more extra beds. There were a lot of decorations and a nice television and refrigerator. Anything you named; we had a house full of nice, expensive items. Many years of living in the same house had allowed me to amass way too much stuff. *We only had one week to sell everything we owned, and we wanted to make as much money as possible.*

First, he didn't pay much for it all. My mom gave me a very vintage gift when I married. But it was very special, not just because it's my mom's gift, because it was from my grandparents. My mom gave each of my sisters and brothers one of our grandparents' vintage items. We were so proud of that, but I tried to give it back to my mom. She didn't want to take it back. She said, "It's from your grandfather's house. I kept it all these years. And after it's been a part of your house, I can't take it back." None of my sisters or brothers wanted to have it because they believed it belonged to me, and I must take it along with me, but I didn't know anything about our mystery trip yet. As I said, we weren't allowed to take anything with us except money, if we had it. No one knew, either, where we were going or how long we were flying, so I decided to leave some of my valuable stuff with my middle sister.

My husband and I always liked to go shopping for our cozy home. We never tried to save money. We both continued with each other. He cared about our needs. I cared about him and the kids, and our house. We both tried to make our life happy, simple, and exciting.

Oh, I forgot to talk about my two beautiful rugs I had. They were called Kermanshah rugs, made in Persia. It was a very expensive type of rug. For all these good things, after all negotiations, the guy gave us a very little amount of money. He knew we must sell things because we must leave in one week, and we didn't have enough time. He also knew we needed money.

When you are having a difficult time, it's the best time to know real people around you. This is very important to know. Life is all about lessons and experience. In these few days, after we put our home up for sale, we discovered a lot of things about people. We knew who our real friends were and who cared about us, but that wasn't the case. We were having a very tough time. We didn't know what was next. We just lived our life day by day, not sure about anything. It was confusing. It was scary, full of emotion. Leaving our country and going to the United States was a big change in our life, and a big tragedy about our life as well.

I wanted to stay at least for a few more years, as I said in the beginning, but we never knew what life was hiding for us, for anybody. Life itself was a big mystery.

I wanted my kids to grow up between my family (my mom and dad, sisters and brothers). I was very close to my family

That day after we made a deal with that guy, he came back in only thirty minutes with his truck and two more guys to help him. In only a few hours, they took everything. I was so sad and angry. I was very emotional. I didn't know what I should do. My husband tried to comfort me. He also was sad and angry, but we couldn't do anything. After the guys left, I had to clean up the house and get ready to leave.

A few minutes before we left the house, my parents showed up to see how we were doing and whether we'd found a good deal for our stuff. But I said to my mom, "Look, we're done, as you see. Look, the house is empty. It's just a cold, empty house. The guy, he came up with this price, as you know. We don't have much time, so we must accept the deal." I was telling my mom what had happened and was crying very hard, with all my heart. My mom and dad cried with me too. We knew it was a big bargain. My parents were shocked when they knew we sold everything we owned, for very little money. They were both surprised at how greedy people were, trying to take advantage of people in our situation, who needed money more than anything else. We were going on the mystery trip. My mother was very sad. She looked at me with her tearing eyes and said, "Oh my God, baby," and she hugged me again and again. I said, "Don't cry, Mom. If we will be safe…it's all about our safety." My heart was tearing apart.

She said, "You're right, baby, you're right. I want you to be positive. We want you all to be safe. God bless your heart." She tried to stop crying and hide her tears, and then she tried to comfort me. She said, "Oh, this all can be replaced even better. When you go to America, you can buy everything even better, made in USA." She said that with a big smile.

And we all tried to make the situation better and funnier, but nobody was laughing from their heart. We all faked it, but my parents want us to be more positive and not think about our stuff. I wanted them to think that I was not sad anymore and I would try to accept the fact, even if it wasn't fair. We left our house and took only our luggage.

My husband closed the door, and we headed to my parents' house. I was laughing and faking it well, but inside my heart, I was feeling that I had been cut into pieces and my heart was bleeding the whole time for our life with my family.

I didn't have any words to say to my parents to make them not worried about me. I couldn't lie to them; just like now, I can't explain how I was feeling at that time. I can't say I was sad because *sad* is not the right word, and not enough to explain the pain inside me. I'm still crying when I'm writing these memories. They were very hard days in my life; it felt more like an end to our life! It was something else, something hard to explain.

My dad asked if we wanted to stay at their house, or if we had somewhere else to go. I said, "Yes, we are staying at your house." He looked at me very sadly and said, "Welcome, my sweetheart. you can stay as long you want."

I said, "Thank you, Dad. We will only stay three days, and then we will leave." I said that, and I was looking at my dad's eyes and again put a fake smile on my face. My dad smiled back at me. He started talking to my husband, and he said, "If anything happens, or anything doesn't go right, you guys always can come back to my house, we always welcome you."

My husband said, "Thank you. This is very nice of you. What could happen, do you think?" he asked my dad

My dad said, "I hope nothing bad happens, but I'm just saying just in case, my house is always open for you, my daughter, and your kids."

After I heard that from my dad, I was thinking about what just he said! Then I said to myself, "What possibly can happen after we sold our home and gave up our life, with all our good and bad memories? No, nothing is going to happen after all that." I kept thinking about what my dad said.

It was a very confusing time. I didn't know how I should be. Should I be sad or happy?

Sometimes I wished we could have stayed at least one more year to spend more time with my family, my sisters and brothers. Every one of my family members had the best time ever with us. We loved to be surrounded by our families.

We also liked to be happy. Helping people isn't just positive for other people; it makes our lives better and happier. My husband and I always opened our door and our hearts for our family and friends because we believed that helping others gave us a sense of purpose and satisfaction. They hoped we could stay in Kurdistan and not leave them, that we wouldn't go anywhere. They loved us even more than we thought, but of course no one could ask us to stay, because it was an unknown condition.

During that hard time, we were getting ready to leave Kurdistan. I thought about the way we were leaving the country. They were basically kicking us out of our own country. It wasn't the way we wanted to leave. We were in a situation that we had to leave even sooner. We loved Kurdistan to death.

To me, it was like taking my soul from my body. How can you live without your heart? I felt like I was between life and death. How could I leave all my memories here in my country and start a new chapter somewhere without my family? How could I live without my life? We'd had a dark childhood, but we survived together and fought together, because we had been together. We helped and supported each other, but now how could I start in a very different country without my family? I was shaking just thinking about that. It was just something I couldn't imagine!

I wanted to enjoy my life with my family, especially when my dad was seventy-eight years old. I wanted to be with him and my mom if they needed me. I wanted my kids to grow up with my family. I wanted them to learn from my father how to be tough and strong but sweet and kind at the same time. How to be soft and brave, just like my mom. She has many different types of personalities. My mom was active with the group of (patriotic union of Kurdistan) PUK back to 1972 or maybe earlier. I remember when my mom had a meeting with a group of women and men at our house. I was only a little girl sneaking around to know what was going on. What have they been talking about inside that room? My mom was using that room for her meeting with her secret group, because it was our biggest, nicest room in the house. We used that room only for our guests for special events or holidays.

But one day my mom caught me! Later she took me aside and put her hand on my shoulder and shook me very hard with anger. She was very serious when she yelled at me and said, "Look at me!" with a very angry voice. "Look in my eyes." Then she yelled again. "Never, ever tell anyone, anything, about what you know what you saw today, never, OK?" I was looking at my mom's face, but I couldn't talk back to her. I was so terrified of her. She was so upset. "Did you hear me? Answer me." I said, "I don't know anything," and I started crying. I was so scared; I didn't know why my mom wanted to hide her guests and why she was so serious about them. Why she was so scared if I told anyone? We always had guests in our house, family and friends, sometimes neighbors, but why? My mom never hid them from anyone. That was the real question I asked myself. I didn't know exactly what was going on at that time. But my mom was very sad and emotional that day, I remember. She was also very angry. When I said I didn't know anything, I was telling her the truth, but after I saw her eyes was so angry, I didn't want to know anything.

Many years later, after I grew up enough, I knew why my mom hid everyone. She was working with a PUK group. That day she knew that one of the very important people in her cell had been killed, but that day I promised my mom that I wasn't going to tell anything to anyone in my life. And I did, so I wanted my daughter to be just like my mom, a brave, strong lady who loyal, and loved her country. My dad was a very thoughtful, intelligent, and hard worker too.

Everything happened in a very short time. After a few days, we were ready to leave.

We know we were surrounded by many wonderful people who were caring for us. We never wanted to sell our lovely home to anybody if something like that wasn't happening. We decided to stay, but this is what happened. We must leave; everyone in my family felt so sorry for us, but no one knew how exactly I feel! The guy gave us only $3,000 for everything! It was only the value of my living room and bedroom. He took advantage of us at that time. But we didn't care as much as our safety. We were worried about our kids and our lives. We just needed enough money to get out of the country. I only took some of clothes for my kids and us for the United States because they kept saying that the process would be very fast, and we don't need a lot of clothes. Maybe it would take a week or ten days at the longest to get there USA, so we try to minimize the luggage.

After everything was done and sold, the only thing left it was three bags of clothes for my kids, my husband, and me, and one plate from my grandparents' house, with a little money that we got from our stuff. That day, when we went to my father's house, it blew me away; it was another dark page of my life.

We went to my parents' house; all my sisters and brothers came over with their kids and their spouses. After we had a big dinner, we tried to have a good time together; they tried to make it fun because we only had two more night with them! Maybe we would never see each other or would never get together again. Who knew what may happen! My brother said, "Why are you guys sad? A lot of people just like you guys are having a party now every night with their families. A lot of people are paying a thousand dollars just to get out and go anywhere, not America! You guys are going to the greatest country ever and are sad? I don't understand why you guys are not happy." He kept talking like that, and he tried to make me happy. He was hugging me and talking to me, joking. I knew why he did that, but I was so quiet. My mom and my sisters were also very quiet. My brother looked at the whole situation in a very different way; he was still a student in the college, he was still young. He thought that when he graduated, he would leave the country. Everybody knew there was no future in our country because of Saddam. He was so happy that we were leaving, and we would be safe, but after he finished his speech, he started crying more than anybody else, because he was missing us even though we were still there! Everyone wanted to show us that they were happy for us, but at the end they were so sad and worried for us. That night all my sisters and brothers stayed over at my parents' house.

My brother was very positive about our trip. He kept saying, "Everything is going to be OK" I really wanted to believe him and be happy just like some other families, so I tried to not cry in front of my family, especially my parents, because I knew how they felt. My mom was more patient than me and my dad. She tried to show me that she was happy. She told me many times that we were going to another country, and we would be safe there, but I know she was very worried too. I could see that in her eyes. But my dad looked more worried. Any time I looked at him, he tries to hide his tears from me and put a fake smile on his face.

The last night at my parent house my dad took me aside in his bedroom. "Sit down, sweetheart." I sat on the edge of his bed. He said, "Let me chitchat with you for a little bit, my daughter." Then he took a deep breath. He looked at me. "Listen to me, my girl. You are about to go somewhere that very different from our country, in a four-way, lifestyle, the culture, the language, and the religion. All these differences are huge. Beside there are many kinds of race living there. You must be ready to deal with every type of person. They don't know who you are or where you come from! Also, they don't know much about your religion! They don't know anything about your language. you must learn their language, first to introduce yourself to them and tell them who you are. You are a Kurd. Where you come from and why you are there! My daughter, you need to learn their culture, to know how to survive, and to be able to live with them, and work with them. Then, if they ask you about your religion, don't be afraid to tell them the truth. Tell them you're a human being first, then a good person as a Muslim. If they asked you what you believe in, tell them we believe in one God that created all of us. And we believe in the three messengers that God sent to all people to leave together in peace and love each other. We believe in Moses, Jesus, and Muhammad. When the time passes, day by day, you will be one of them."

I was listening to my dad carefully. Whatever my dad said was fact. He also said, "My girl, be happy, be positive. Don't worry, sweetheart. This life is all about surprises. Give and take. Don't be disappointed when it takes from you. You will get it back maybe better in a different way, but be happy, and thank God for everything. Trust your God. Maybe God has a better life planned for your family. We never know until we try. Stop crying. That is not good for your eyes and your heart. Try to be ready for new life; it will happen soon."

He hugged me and I kissed him. I told him, "Thank you, Dad. I will promise you that I will do my best, and I will make you happy and proud of me." I was trying to be very positive. He squeezed my hand, and he stood up. He went to the living room where my mom and sister and brother were. I was still thinking of his speech when he came back to his room. He called me. "My girl, I always pray for you and your family to be safe whenever you go. I love you so much."

I told him, "I love you, too, Dad."

After a few minutes, he came back to me. He said, "You don't have to say goodbye tomorrow morning when you leave, OK, baby? I don't like to say goodbye."

I said, "OK, Daddy, as you like." It was so sudden! But I knew why my dad said that. I said to him, "Then I'm not even hugging you again. Just go to bed and sleep, my dearest dad."

But he looked at me, and this time he couldn't stop his tears. And with a very broken voice full of pain, he said, "Good luck;

have a nice trip. Take care of yourself and your kids and your husband." He went to his room.

I tried to go to the living room, where everyone was sitting quietly. They looked sleepy too. It had been a long day and long night for all of us. I wanted tomorrow to come fast and leave. I wanted to stop all this drama. I called my mom and said, "Mom, please go to bed. I know my dad is having a hard time. I know he can't sleep but go talk to him. Tell him we will be OK." At that minute, I was very worried about my dad. The whole time he hid his emotions from us, but I saw him many times when he was looking at my kids and his eyes were full of tears that he didn't release. He was very panicked. He was moving around the house, going from one room to another. We all noted that, so finally he went to his bed. I hoped he had fallen asleep.

Chapter 12

The whole time, everyone was acting. I didn't know we all could be actors. I knew life was like a big theater and we were acting. Everyone acts in their own way; everyone has their own character. We'd been very good actors—my dad, my mom, me, my sisters and brothers. We all had been acting for each other. They were acting like they were happy for us and that we would be OK, and I was acting that I was cool and happy, but, I wasn't happy, and neither were they. They were worried, just like me and Dad.

But no matter how good your acting is, reality is coming up, and the fake is going away. The truth was very clear. I was so scared of that minute; I wished everybody could leave without saying goodbye. That night my kids had a lot of fun with their cousins. My daughter asked me if I would allow her to stay with my parents. That way she could always see her cousins and play with them. I told her, "No, sweetheart, you can't. You must be with us, and we would miss you if you stayed here." I couldn't explain it more than this to her, but she started crying and begging me because she had a very good time with her cousins. That night was very tough, making my family believe that we were happy about going to the United States. That was not easy to prove, to make my kids believe that we would try to come back as soon we could. It was just difficult, because I wasn't happy; I had a broken heart. Our lives did not belong to us. It was like that: if you stayed, you got killed; if you left, you stayed alive. When you are between two choices, life or death, of course we picked life—if not for us, for the kids.

That night I felt a fire inside my heart. It was burning me, cutting me to the pieces. I also felt I was such a pathetic person. I couldn't do anything about it; when my kids were so happy and loved being with their cousins but were not allowed to have that fun anymore. When I was looking at them they were happy, playing and calling each other's names, giggling and laughing together, it was such a miserable time for me. I asked myself, *why? Why are my kids not allowed to grow up in their own country? Why not?* I was asking myself the same question over and over. We both had worked hard to have a decent life for our kids. But now we had nothing—just $3,000 and three bags. That was all.

The same night after we become homeless, a lot of my friends and my husband's friends came over to my parent house to say goodbye. My aunts and uncles, and my cousins and their families, came for the same reason. Everyone wished us good luck as we hugged everyone and said goodbye. They all left, but my sisters and brothers stayed over with us. The kids went to bed, and we remained awake in the living room until the next day. Nobody slept that night.

The taxicab was there at 5:00 a.m. We were ready. I wanted to leave without hugging or saying goodbye to anyone, especially my mom and dad. Everyone was trying to avoid this moment, because all of us were very emotional. The past weeks, I had tried to keep all my emotion to myself and not show my family how I felt about everything.

My sisters and brothers were very strong and supportive. They tried to make me feel like I was going to vacation; they tried to make everything easy and good. They told me I should be happy and thankful. The words always helped me and gave me courage. But in my heart, it looked like the end of the world. I couldn't stop thinking about my family for one minute, even though my husband and kids were with me. I had a feeling that I would not see my parents again.

We left my parents' house at six o'clock in the morning on Wednesday, December 4, 1996. We headed to Erbil, Duhok, and then to Zaxo. That was the plan. These are all Kurdish cities. It took us about seven hours driving to get to Zaxo to the north Kurdistan. We stopped a few times on the way to Zaxo, because of my kids. We got to Zaxo in the afternoon. The weather was cold and rainy; we were hungry and tired, so we stopped at a restaurant to eat. The food wasn't good, my husband and I couldn't eat that food so we both decided to look for another restaurant. We both were tired and sad and still hungry! The kids looked sleepy; they fell asleep a few times in the car.

I'd been thinking about everything in the past weeks, and now here we are, going to face the mystery of our future. Maybe it is a good thing, maybe it is not. Who knows? We were going without knowing what was waiting for us.

I tried to convince myself that this is a fact. I must accept it, and I'm not alone. There were many people there, too, just like me, leaving their families. I knew everyone had a different idea; people are different. Some people were not thinking like I did. Some couldn't wait to get to the United States; they were very happy. Some didn't want to leave the country but were still happy! Some didn't care about anything. They just wanted to leave. Maybe they didn't have a good family like I did; they didn't have anyone to miss, but I was thinking over and over. The whole time I asked myself why I couldn't stop thinking about that terrible event and think about a new future with my kids and husband. Why? I wanted to be happy just like the others. I was crying most of the time. I wanted to be more realistic, and I told myself many times I had to accept this because it was happening.

Now we got to Zaxo, and in two days we would pass the Kurdistan border into Turkey. I knew I didn't have much luck in life, but I hoped this time, I would have a little, at least for my kids. I believe life is about opportunity. Sometimes it brings you good chances. I wanted good luck for my kids.

After driving around that small city, we finally found a decent place to take a rest also my kids want to eat again, soon we sat. We asked for food and drinks. The kids were so hungry and tired after long hours in the car.

My kids finished eating, and I changed my son; he was messy after he ate. As we were getting ready to leave the restaurant, we meet another family there, our friends. We were surprised to see them in that restaurant because we thought they had already left the country, but they said they had left the same day as us, so it was nice to have some friends with us on our unknown trip to a big country like the United States.

They asked us if we knew a good hotel around this area. We told them yes, so they deiced to go with us. We all left and went to the hotel together with our friends. They had two kids, one girl, one boy, almost the same age as my kids. I hoped they would be good company for my kids and keep them too busy to talk about their cousins and grandparents.

The hotel we went to be a five-star hotel; it was just a hotel in a small city. It was packed. I think it was the only hotel in that city, because it was full of people from my city (Sulaymaniyah) and another city like Erbil. The hotel was nice, clean, and organized. We only wanted to stay for a few days until our departure; we would go to Ibrahm khalil first and then to Turkey. Ibrahm khalil is a small checkpoint between Kurdistan and Turkey. When we arrived at the hotel, we saw a lot of people who were ready to leave the next day.

The hotel was crowded with the people everywhere: the rooms, the restaurant, the lobby. Everywhere was crowded. People were busy getting ready to cross the country. Every day one or two groups of a different organization were crossing the country. I met a lot of families that I knew them a long time ago, but I was surprised that many families were leaving our country. I never imagined that I would meet those people again, especially in that hotel.

The first night away from my family was a very hard night for me, but I tried to get some sleep. We hadn't slept the night before. We thought we would be very tired, and we could sleep after a long day, but after I saw all these busy people, I knew it will be hard even close our eyes. We went to our room on the second floor. I thought maybe our room could be a little quieter than the first floor, but everywhere was the same.

Our room wasn't as clean as I thought. I wanted to give a bath to kids and myself; then we can get some sleep. I gave my daughter and my son a very quick bath, because the water was cold, and the hotel was cold too. Too many people were using the showers at the same time because they were leaving tomorrow. We knew it was not going to be easy. I said to my husband, "We can wait until tomorrow. I know most of them are leaving tomorrow morning." He said, "Yes, we can wait. I'm so tired; I really want to sleep. Please turn the light off." While we had that small talk, the kids had already fallen asleep.

I couldn't sleep that night. There was a lot of noise, people talking in the lobby, calling each other. They were trying to get ready for tomorrow morning to leave. I heard the third group of people should leave the hotel at 7:00 a.m. the next day. I think maybe I fell asleep for one or two hours. My husband was awake most of the time.

The room next door had a family leaving at 7:00 a.m. She was rushing her kids to be ready starting at 4:00 a.m. She yelled at them, saying, "Hurry up, we don't have enough time! We don't want to be left behind. The bus will be here at six a.m., not at seven o'clock." When I heard that, it was so funny for me, because somebody didn't believe they were finally getting out and leaving the country forever.

What was sad was that I didn't want to leave, but we were not able to stay in our country either. So that night I couldn't stop thinking about the way we were living, and everything came back to my mind. I didn't think anyone could sleep that night. My eyes were open most of the time. I heard the voices coming closer to our room. Somebody knocked at the door and said, "You don't want to say goodbye to us? Get up; nobody can sleep here."

She called my name twice. At first, I thought they were talking to my next-door neighbor, but she called me one more time and knocked on the door again. She said, "Shereen, open the door! We are leaving now. Sleep when you get to America."

I jumped on my bed and went to open the door. When I did, I saw two of my friends. They were not that close to me, but we knew each other long time ago. They were dressed very nicely with a lot of makeup! They dressed like they had a party or something. I look at them and said, "Really, you guys are leaving now?"

She said, "Yes, madam," in a very happy and funny voice. She said, "We are leaving now. The bus is here. We just want to say bye and see you guys there in America." She asked me when we were going, tomorrow or today. I said I'm not sure.

I hugged them both, and I wished a safe trip for them and said, "Yes, see you there." And they left quickly. After they left, I shut the door. My husband was awake and asked me who are they? and if I knew them. I said, "Yes, I know them, but I'm surprised how they are going to America and their husbands are not working in any of the organizations! They asked me when our turn is. I said, 'I'm not sure. I think my husband said we are the last group, or maybe before the last one.'"

My husband said, "I don't understand these people. Yesterday they were sad and miserable. But now they sound very happy."

I said, "Yes, I just remember they were crying when I saw them first time. They looked very sad. It looks like they came with somebody, but they didn't let them go. How did I forget that? How did I forget to ask them how they can leave now?" After a long talk about that strange thing that happened, we woke up the kids to get to go eat breakfast, and I said, "So what if they like to go to the United States? Why not? I'm happy for them. So, what? if five thousand people are leaving now? Let's become five thousand and two."

But my husband said, "No, that is not right; it shouldn't be this way. Who knows how many more crossed without paper or real IDs? And what else will happen after that? We don't know yet. Now they are leaving—how did that happen?" He looked at me with surprise.

"It's sad, I know. There was another lady. She can't take her own kids with her because her kids are twenty and twenty-three years old and they are married, so they are not allowed to go according to the traveling policy and rules of the United States. They already had their own families," I said. "But I saw her. She was happy. She didn't look worried or sad."

He said, "But her husband said to me, they must leave their own son in Kurdistan, because they are married, so they can't go to America. That is what the rule said." In that minute I felt something was not right. I don't remember why. Maybe because we knew something about the traveling policy, but we saw something different. That day I felt something big was going to happen. I had never had that weird feeling in my life. Maybe I was wrong. Maybe I was just thinking too much, so I tried to take my kids to downstairs to the hotel restaurant to have breakfast. We left the room, and my husband went with his friends to say goodbye.

My kids and I tried to spend more time in the hotel with the other families. We met a lot of new, good people there, and we made good friends in three days. We promised to find each other in America if we went to different states.

After only a few hours, many families started to leave the country after checking their IDs and where they worked. They were asked which organization they had worked with and how many members were in their family. Some of them had more questions they'd been asked at the station checkpoint in Zaxo. They sent them out on big buses to Ibrahm khalil and then to Turkey.

That day we stayed at the hotel with many other families. It was a cold, windy, rainy day. No one had any information about this evacuation except Turkey. Turkey let the Kurdish people stay in their land, not inside the city, but somewhere in the north, we had heard. So, America built a big camp for Kurdish people to stay only for a few days until they transferred to Guam, United States. The rule of the evacuation was very clear and simple. All employees of the American organization and their families must leave Kurdistan as soon as possible. If the father in the family was employed, he should take his wife and his underage kids. But a single employee could take his or her parents only, not siblings. There was a big list of the employees' names who worked with American organizations, and the names of their families.

It was a very emotional time for most of the families. People brought their older kids, but they didn't know if the people in charge would let them pass with their families or not. They still had hope that maybe they would.

They did help them; they could pass with the whole family together and happy. We didn't know how! We saw how they left the country and were satisfied, but some families couldn't take any extra people with them, even if they were their kids. We went to the station one day just to see the process. We saw a lot of people who were very happy, and more were very sad. I was happy when I saw somebody smiling and happy, when they didn't leave anyone of his or her family behind. They finally survived.

I heard and I saw a lot of heartbreaking stories, in the hotel. People talked about whom they had left behind and what they had lost. It was a feeling I'd never had before, because I was always thinking about my problem. I thought I was the only one with a family, I was the only one missing my country, I was the only one missing good days and beautiful times in my life. I thought I was the only one who would never see my mom and dad again, but that day I realized I was not the only one. People were leaving their own kids. That was hurt. I was between those people listening to their stories; I forgot mine. I was crying with them; for the first time, I wasn't crying for myself. Wow, I really felt bad for those new friends I met at the hotel.

I had left all my family and all my friends behind, after I lost everything, I had, after I gave up on my life to follow the unknown journey with my husband and my kids. I just thought for the first time that I had to be happy for my kids to survive after all, so I did this for my kids' better future, for a safer life.

I was sad. I already missed my mom and dad, my siblings and their kids. But I knew that we would meet again sometime. When? After how many years? But I knew it would happen. I just prayed that all my family stayed alive and healthy. I hoped that I would see them again in another, better time. I was talking to myself the whole time, but after I met those, sad miserable people, I started talking to them about my experience. We were alike, similar in many ways, like our life in the past and our life in the present. We talked about many things that were happening in our lives, because we all came from the same place, and we belonged to the same country. Now we were at the same hotel, and we had the same plan.

We became a big family there. We shared our experiences, and we exchanged our ideas about what we knew and where to go. We were going to another country together; maybe we would make another, different live together, safer and full of excitement.

After all, I was the one who was telling them maybe it was the end of our difficult life. We should be happy. Maybe it's a very good things happening now just like my brother said—if not for us, at least for our kids.

For a few days while we were at the hotel, my husband and his friend went out with every group that was leaving. We were staying with our kids and waiting for the order to tell us to be ready, with the day and the time. Every group has a one or two person who was taking care of the organizing the families. what they did was

They had everyone's name. They made a group. They organized everything; they tried to make it easy. We just needed to be there at the right day and time. They sent the people according to the list; that list came from Bill Clinton, the president of the United States of America in 1996, after Saddam announced he was about execute all these people who worked with American organizations.

In our culture, it is difficult to leave your kids behind even if they are overage, because kids stay with their parents until they are married. So that was a very tough decision for some families to leave their kids behind and leave the country. Because some families' kids' names weren't on that list, they couldn't go. They must stay in Kurdistan, even if their father or mother worked with Americans. Saddam didn't care whether he or she is older or married. With Saddam's crazy adoptions, Kurdistan was very dangerous for all these who were American employees and their families as well.

We spent one more day in the hotel. My kids were busy playing with the other kids. Sometimes they were bored, and they wanted to do something else besides sitting and painting in the hotel room or at the hotel cafeteria. I took a lot of colored pencils and sketches with me for my daughter; she always liked to draw pictures. She was a very talented kid, and she liked to play with Barbie dolls. I took some of them for her too. My son was only two and half years old; he didn't know much, but he had started speaking early. He was trying to hold a pencil and draw something just like his sister, but he couldn't do anything, just scribbling. Sometimes we laughed at him a lot. We asked him, "What is this?" He didn't know what it was, so he got angry and threw the pencil away. Then he started crying.

I hid my face when I started laughing at him; he was so cute and funny. If we laughed at him hard, he cried harder; he got so embarrassed. Oh, my baby, I loved him so much. Then I had to hug him and tell him how he was a very good painter, and then he stopped crying. I took his car toys for him to play with, but he was greedy. He didn't want to share his toys with anyone. Anyway, I had a good time when I was watching them there busy together; at least they didn't ask me to go back to visit Grand mom and Grandpa.

That night my friend she came to our room, she asked me if I'd like to join the rest of the families there at the hotel cafeteria? because they decided to have a nice party before our mystery trip begin, we didn't know if we can meet again! Or where we go next after Guam, we needed to have a good time together to make a good memory, since we were living tomorrow.

Some of us we have been friend long time ago, but some of them we just get to meet at that hotel, then we became a good friend, especially our kids. It was our last night together, I said

OK to my friend; let's do it, and make some fun, I'm sure our kids they love to have fun, they needed, so after a few minutes we went downstairs to meet the other families who were left for the last trip with us.

My kids were very energetic and happy with their new friends. I heard my daughter start asking questions about America. "Where are we going in America? What will we do there? Where will we live? Are we going to school again? What will America look like?" Question after question. I think after all she got excited because my daughter was a very social kid; she easily could make friends. That was a good thing. It made me happy; I think she was ready to move on and be a happy kid again.

After we had a good time with those families, we wanted to have a good dinner again for the last time at the same restaurant we had been before. It was the only nice restaurant in that small city. Most of the people there were going for lunch and dinner every day to that restaurant to eat, because it was clean, and their food was delicious. After we done eating, we went back to the hotel to our room, to get ourselves ready for our trip. I started to put everything in the luggage to get ready for the next day. We didn't have a lot of stuff with us, just a few clothes and some items we needed. I tried to give my son and daughter a bath and let them sleep because we must be in the lobby next day at 6:00 a.m. We went to bed earlier than normal because we knew that tomorrow we would have a long day. I tried to sleep but I couldn't. I tried to think about nice, bright features; I tried to be more positive; my husband was already failing asleep and start snoring, and my kids were asleep too. I was worried, panicked. I knew it was over. I was asking myself why I wasn't happy? I thought I should just be like the others. So, it was a very long night for me again.

My alarm went off at 5:00 a.m. I jumped on my bed. I saw my kids; they were awake and my husband too. I think I had just fallen asleep, but it was too late for me to sleep. I had to get up, to get ready in one hour and leave the hotel.

We went downstairs to the cafeteria. We saw our old and new friends there. They were already start their breakfast they looked much happier than before. I think everybody looked like they had gotten over their difficulties and were ready for our new journey. I saw that those people were looking brighter than before. I think after they knew the time was already here and we were only a few days away from America, they tried to convince themselves that this is happening now. Even if we refused in the beginning to leave our country like that, but now we know the only truth: which is our country was not for us anymore.

We must leave, whether we liked it or not! Or we faced another truth, which was to be executed by Saddam's regime. We tried to not talk about that past anymore, only our futures. I thought for a minute. Maybe we are very lucky people! Why not? We are going to America, and this is America! The talk was about anything, just to pass the time, but most of our talk was about America. We didn't know much about this big country, and we couldn't imagine how our lives would be there. It was just like a mystery.

I was so unhappy; it was like something hard coming my way. I didn't know how to explain it; only God knew what it was all about. I prayed in my heart that God would keep us safe. I had all my luggage ready, my kids, and my husband. I usually put some food for my kids in my backpack just in case, because we didn't know how many hours we need to get to the Turkish border, so I brought food and water. Even my husband yelled at me, but I didn't listen to him, right? We heard it was about ten hours' driving; I knew we lived in a country that always we must expect shocks. I had a lot of surprises from my past, but now I even have more in my present. I thought I had enough for all my life, but I was wrong. I didn't see much.

For the first time in my life, I got to know a lot of people, good and bad. I can't say *bad* because there wasn't enough time to really know people, and the time was going fast, but I can say they were weird. Everybody was busy, confused, sad, angry, and tired. Some of them were happy; some had lost direction about their lives. Some believe their lives had just started; some felt that this is the end for them. It was hard to understand what life was about. Should you die in your country with your family? Or keep going and look for your destiny wherever and however? Or just be happy, be positive, and go with flow, or believe that one day will be better than today? Which one was right for us? No one could answer that.

We all were confused. Some believed that when they got to America, they would make money and they would buy everything they want and better, or maybe the American government would give them money, so they didn't care what they lost. And many more had ideas that Americans would take us to a laboratory to do experiments on Kurds or to use us in their farms like slaves. We heard a lot of strong opinions from different people; it was good and horrible experience at the same time.

Three days usually not enough to know people, but I think a bad condition can express to you the real person. I was so angry, but everything was going fast. Everyone wanted first to be survived; we all were in the same dangerous position. Everywhere I went, I learned something from people's experiences. I knew the biggest lessons we always learn from our own lives, who we're meeting during our time life, where we are working at, the places we've been, the wired situation we are going throw After all, we have a purpose in our life. My life's purpose was to be saved and be happy with my family. Here I was, trying to be in a safe place with my family; some people can get a good benefit from that. I learned about many different types of people— good people give you happiness, bad people give you experience, worse people give you lessons, I get to know selfish and caring, kind and hard. Basically, I can say good and bad, they have been an important part of our life.

To me life is like a big school. Learning from life is difficult but it's more important to learn from school itself.

After fifteen minutes the bus was there in front of the hotel. The families came one by one; the kids were happy and laughing together. The bus driver yelled and said, "Hurry up, guys; let the kids in first. Bring food for the kids. I will not stop on the way to the station; I know you guys have a lot of kids." He was right; we had about ten kids just between five families. Then maybe after twenty to thirty minutes, everybody was on the bus and ready to leave. We left and headed to the station. We got there after almost thirty minutes. The bus stopped. Everybody was so quiet; the kids still were sleepy, but happy. For the first time since long ago, I felt I was happy because of my kids, and we were finally ready to leave and start a new journey.

The driver said, "Here we are. Now one of you should go and tell them that you are from that organization and show them your paper to let you go." So, my husband and one of his friends went inside that building. The paper they had inside that office should have all information about everyone, and we had same paper as well, at the same time they had a power to let the people through.

First, they needed to check our IDs to make sure which company we belonged to. That was because they already had information about everyone; then they were supposed to leave us to go. My husband and his friend went inside that building. There was a small room with a patio, and it had a small window where you can't see much inside the room from outside. I think I saw three men with uniform sitting there; we didn't know who they are, but I'm sure they were a people who had a power, and they were important.

My husband went inside with one of his friends after he introduced himself to them, He showed them his ID and the list he had in his hand with everyone's names, because we all belonged to the same American organization GDC. I was sitting beside the window on that bus. I could see my husband's face but not much. We couldn't hear anything, but somehow, I saw my husband; he was talking to them, and they had one of the guys. He had a paper in his hand. He stood up and was talking to my husband. I still can see his face! But it was not clear; I felt something was not right. I started to pay more attention to what is going on. But nothing looks clear to me, He was talking, but obviously we couldn't hear anything. We were still waiting inside the bus with a lot of noises from kids. twenty minutes passed. We were still in the bus and waiting; the kids and ladies were very loud. Everyone was talking and laughing. We didn't know what was going on inside. I start worried because; my husband had been inside the office more than thirty minutes, suddenly one of the guys inside the bus said, "I'm going to see what is in going on." At that minute my husband and his friend got out. They came back to the bus; he looked angry and worried. He looked at me. He said, "Give me Alan" (my son). I gave him Alan; he was sitting on my lap. After he held him, we waited him to tell us what took him that long. Everyone was waiting for him to say something. Why was he acting weird.? It was like he didn't know how to tell us what was happening there, so I said "What took you that long there? Is everything OK?"

He looked at me with the worried face and looked at the others and said, "No, nothing's OK. We are not going anywhere. We are not allowed to pass, right now!" with a very shaking voice

First, no one understood what he was talking about. One of his friends said, "You're joking, right?" with a smile. He said, "No, I'm serious; we are not going to America." And he handed the paper he had in his hand to his friend and said, "Look what they did to our name."

I said, "Tell us what they said to you." He tried to explain to us, but everyone yelled at him, like he was responsible for what happened, again he tries to tell them what happened, no one listened. We all had a big shock, and we all yelled asked aquation everyone was talking and some start crying and suddenly everyone was quiet for a minute or two, but quickly everyone started asking the same questions together at the same time, over and over because that was the last thing we wanted to hear.

In that minute, nobody wanted to hear that. What he said was so problematic. Just thirty minutes earlier, everything was great. And now he said exactly the opposite of what we were about to do! How did that happen? We did not understand why. So, every single one asked the same questions over and over. What? What? Why? How? We all couldn't get what he was telling us; he kept repeating it over and over. We didn't believe what he was telling us.

Everyone started arguing with him and was angry; they were asking him questions, like whether he was responsible for what happened! But he just was shocked like anybody else, and he argued with those guys inside that office, but they said they had another new list that didn't have our names on it. So, they said they couldn't do anything with this; it was an order from the top security. If your name is not on this list, you are not allowed to pass this border. Just for one minute, everyone stopped talking, and we were thinking again, *Is this real? Is what is happening real?* It was hard and ridiculous when something like this happened in just a few minutes that would change your entire life forever. The hardest part was that we didn't know why. We were powerless; we had no one to tell or explain to us why or how it happened. The only ones we could talk to be those guys at the checkpoint who could not make decisions.

On the real list we had, all our names were there—first and last names and all information about us. We still had that in our hands; everyone had a copy of it. But the list they showed my husband, and his friend was totally different. Our name was crossed out with a black pen—eight families from one organization, GED, and a few more people from a different organization! That time was the most disappointing of my life. Everything changed. I got into the situation that I didn't know, what should we believe? Where should we go? I think it's too late to go back home! Because we knew what was waiting for us if we go back to our country! And those people who crossed out our names with a black pen knew exactly what would happen to us if we went back home! but who are they? They were not real human beings. They were murderers. They were that group of people who only cared about their needs and were selfish. They didn't care if Saddam killed all of us—not just us, our kids too! So, our lives were that cheap for them? And who does that? Who can send those kids to

Saddam to kill? No, it can't be real. I was quiet the whole time, I was thinking, *who can do that to us? And why?*

We were still on the bus and trying to think about what was next. What should we do? We were angry, sad, and shocked. No one could think without yelling. We kept arguing about what we should do. Where should we go? Stay or leave? Our friend went back to the office again and again talking to those men inside the building, but nothing happened. They all said, "You should leave and stop bothering us"—without thinking that if we left, what would happen to us? Especially after Saddam had everyone's name after we left the country. We didn't know who was responsible for that, who we should blame. Did the company abandon us? Or the guys from the checkpoint? Or people we used to know and work with? I knew everyone had the same feeling, but it wasn't fear. We were stuck there, our brains blocked, our actions frozen. We kept saying the same thing over and over: "where do we go? How do we survive after we lost our jobs, our houses, and everything we owned? And now if we go back, we will lose our lives for sure!"

The time was almost noon. My husband went back again one more time to make a phone call to his manager in America. But the guy inside the office didn't let him do a phone call because he said there was an eight-hour time difference, so again we had to wait until the manager of GDC would wake up, and then we can talk to him. We wanted to know what we should do after that disaster happened to us.

Finally, we decided to send a fax to him to ask what the reason was for the change. And how could we go back without having any place to go? And what should we do here? Should we wait until they fixed that mistake? or who was responsible for that? We were in danger, and we needed help. That was the fax we sent to America. The only answer we got was waiting for one or two weeks until we tell you what to do (right answer)! We were homeless, jobless, and mindless. We were hanging between the earth and the sky. We had no homes to go to; we had nothing. Just us, each other.

Chapter 13

The time passed. We couldn't make any decisions about whether we should go back home and risk our lives or stay two more weeks. We had money from selling our house and our stuff, but it wasn't that much. We thought we would survive if we went to the United States, and we would be OK now! Everything had gone downhill. Why was it happening to us? Do we deserve that? If we do, then what about the kids? What have they done? I asked myself millions of questions, but I got no answer. It was like another nightmare, we were weak and helpless, most of us were crying, and the kids were hungry; they didn't understand what was going on. They needed to eat. We'd been there almost eight hours, and we couldn't do anything, even when the time was right. My husband couldn't reach the manager of GDC.

My daughter was looking at me. She wiped my tears. She said, "Mom, please don't cry. Just pray like you always do, and we will be OK." I was speechless. She was right. That minute was tough. We couldn't do anything, but we could pray for our lives. We only could pray, "My God, help us from this difficult time. I always remember, my God, but in this time, I've forgotten even my name."

Unacceptable things happened to us, but they happened. When my daughter told me, "Mom, don't cry. Just pray like you always do," from that minute, I never stopped praying in my entire life, even in very good times. Kids started asking for food again; we knew they'd been on the bus all day, and of course they wanted to use the bathroom. we all were on the bus all day with very cold weather.

That made us decide to go back to the same hotel. At least we could eat something because we were very hungry. Also, we needed to get some rest; maybe we would feel better after a long, stressful day, so we all decided to go back to the hotel, to stay in until tomorrow. And then the next day, we would come back to call the management again in the United States.

Maybe tomorrow would bring us better luck and a chance to leave! Until that time, we didn't know what we had to do. We had to wait until we got the answer from the United States, so we had to wait until the next day.

My husband asked the bus driver to take us to the restaurant first; we needed to eat. One of the families was a new married couple. They decided to go back to our city, and not spent one more day in Zaxo. The lady said that her father was very sick when she left, and she was very worried about him. Her husband agreed with her, they said if anything new happened let us to know; they would be back soon. We were all surprised. Nobody responded to them, because everyone had agreed about what we just decided, but after ten minutes, they disagreed, and they didn't want to spend one more day in Zaxo. The conversation started again; they tried to make most of us go back with them to our city. In the beginning, no one wanted to, but one more family started to agree with them. This family had only a six-month-old baby, but the other one had just married and didn't have kids. They didn't lose anything as we did; they been living with their family in their parents' house, so basically their lives had just started. They could go anywhere and start a new life anywhere if they wanted. They knew going back to the country was a big risk. But I knew they had another plan. They said they had a better plan. So, my husband and some other families tried to convince them to not go back and just wait with us a week or two. They didn't want to; they wouldn't listen to anyone. They really got angry, and they wanted to go back.

I was very worried about them. I said, "What if you guys go back and they get you and kill you all? You are making a big mistake. If you are not thinking about yourself, at least think about your parents. If they were ill or complaining about some health problem, they will become better with some medicine, but if you get killed by Saddam, you will kill your father; he will die because of you. You are not helping your parents. Please don't do it; just stay with us."

I said, "we need to stay together; we need to know why this happened and how? We had the right to know. Whatever the reason, they should tell us and fix it today, not tomorrow, or we could not go back like this. No house, no job—where should we go?" I knew our family would be more than happy to help us, but our lives were in danger. How long could we hide ourselves from Saddam's men? They would look until they found us. I would never risk my kids' and family's lives. I was talking to them, but they hadn't changed their minds about going back home. I kept saying that what happened was not right, something went wrong:

"Guys, we need to think about this. The people who were just in the same hotel two days ago are now on their way to the United States. Why do we have to go back? This is impossible. Something is wrong. This is not fair; I will not let my kids be left behind."

In that minute I decided no matter what happened, my family had to go to the United States, just like the other kids. I promised myself to do everything for my kids' futures. I knew that somebody was behind that; I knew that was a dirty plan.

We stopped talking because everyone was busy thinking about their next step. I was looking outside the window. It was already dark and raining; the day was a cold, cloudy, ugly day. That bad weather didn't help us relax for a little bit; it was making our mood go from bad to worse. I jumped on my seat when the driver yelled and said, "We are here! Everyone, go eat. I'm going to eat and pray. I didn't pray all day. See you in one hour." He walked away.

We all got down from the bus and went inside the restaurant. We sat with two more families that were our close friends. We tried to look normal, but we couldn't hide that sadness we had. Everyone was quiet. The waiter came and asked us what we wanted to eat. (They didn't have a menu). So, he told us what they had, and we ordered something for the kids and us. We finished eating. After forty-five minutes, the driver came back and said, "I'm ready if you guys are ready." We were ready too. The two other families wanted to leave at the same night, so they left. We wished them a safe trip and good luck.

Surprise after surprise. We all went back to the same hotel, but when we arrived, our rooms had been taken by new people. The hotel was full again. We thought we were the last group, but no, we were not last. There were a lot of people still coming to Zaxo. they will leave in a few days. That made us wonder again why we were not allowed to leave and why our names were crossed out. So now we were at the hotel, and we couldn't stay there because all the rooms were taken. We had to look for another hotel.

We got back on a bus and the driver took us around the city to look for another place to stay. We didn't find anywhere to stay. That city was very small, so we went back to the restaurant again just to ask people if they knew of any place for rent until tomorrow morning. Then my husband and I decided to stay with the group wherever we went, since we were having the same problem. Luckily the restaurant wasn't very crowded. The waiter came quickly to us and asked why we had come back again.

He asked if we were still hungry, with a smile on his face. He also asked why we were still here and not on our way to the US. I said sharply, "Yes, you're right. We shouldn't be here now, but something happened. We don't know yet!" He looked surprised. I said, "We came back for something else, but since we are here, we can drink tea. I have a headache" we used to drink tea in my country three times a day, so everyone asked for tea. The time was near 8:00 p.m.

He said, "Sure, what is the other thing? Maybe I can help you."

My husband said to him, "Do you know if anybody in this area by chance has any room or house for rent until tomorrow? You know, the time is getting late, and we don't have anywhere to go. As you see, the kids are very tired and sleepy. Please tell us if you know anywhere. We are four families. We have eight kids and a pregnant lady too."

While my husband was talking to the waiter, and we were all waiting for him to tell us good news, I saw a guy coming closer to my husband. He was looking at me, but I didn't recognize him.

He got closer and looked at my husband and said, "Hey, man, what are you doing here?"

My husband jumped at that guy's voice and turned around. He hugged him and said, "What are you doing here?" They started hugging each other and asking about each other; we all were surprised. Who was that guy? It seemed my husband knew him from a long time ago. I tried to focus more, but I couldn't recognize him.

My husband asked me if I knew him. I said, "I don't know; I'm not sure."

They both laughed at me, and he said, "Really? You don't know me?"

I said, "I'm sorry, we are still surprised about what happened today, maybe my brain is not working well."

He smiled and then he said, "I'm sorry. Why? What happened?"

My husband told him something about what happened to us that day.

He said, "Oh, I'm so sorry, but why?" He was shocked, just like us. He felt sorry and wanted to help us. He said, "Now you guys want a place for only tonight or more days?"

My husband said, "Maybe for one or two weeks if it's a good place, and not too expensive. We are not sure how long we need it. Maybe a few days. It depends on how fast we get the answer from America."

The guy said, "Listen, my friend. I have an empty house I wanted to fix and remodel at some point, but it's not in very bad shape. It only has one living room, one bedroom, a small kitchen, and one bathroom. It's a small house, but I guess that will be enough for you guys. Just try to stay until you guys are leaving.

The house is empty, but I can give you some blankets and pillows, just enough for tonight."

I looked at him again. I tried to remember; I knew he looked familiar. "Oh my God," I said. "I remember!" I knew him; yes, he was a friend of my husbands at college. It had been a while—almost ten years since we graduated. He looked so different. He was married with two kids. He was living at the house that he wanted to let us rent for a couple of weeks, but at that time he was living with his parents until he fixed his house.

We followed him to his house. After maybe a twenty-minute drive, he stopped in front of the old house. We couldn't see much because it was dark; besides, we just wanted someplace to stay and rest. Our poor kids were very tired; some of them were already asleep. We waited on the bus until he went inside, and he turned the light on. Then my husband went in. We couldn't wait, we were very cold and tired. We waited until he came back and said, "Come on, bring the kids in. We are taking care of the luggage."

Every lady has at least one kid to take with her inside. The problem was kids were all asleep, so we had to carry them. I went inside the house, but I couldn't see anything. It was dark. My husband took my hand and he said, "This is the living room. All of you ladies with the kids sleep in this room, and we men will use the bedroom" (because the living room was much bigger than the bedroom). When I got inside the living room, I didn't see anything there; it was totally empty. I said, "We can't put our kids on the floor. It's concrete; there's no carpet, no rug, nothing." I was so angry. Everybody was angry; we all tried to control ourselves, but it was very hard to do that. We needed a bed, at least something to put on that cold, hard concrete. Our friend's name was Ali. I asked Ali if he could bring some beds or just a few blankets to put on the floor. He said, "I will bring you everything. Just give me one hour."

We needed them only for the kids, because the house was very cold. It had been raining all day and night. We also needed heat. We had been standing in the middle of the room, not knowing what to do. We kept looking at each other without saying any words; it had been such a long day.

We all sat on that cold floor and waited for Ali and my husband to come back with the stuff we needed for that night and the next morning. They came back with a lot of comfortable blankets and pillows and some dishes and food, water, eggs, milk, and a lot of cookies for our kids. We tried to make ourselves comfortable at least until the next day.

We made some beds for the kids and us ladies. We had one pregnant lady. She was at thirty-two weeks, so we wanted her to be more comfortable than anyone else, but the whole time she was crying because she had pain. My husband and the rest of the men went to the other room to get some sleep. We also wanted to get some sleep too. The time was about 12:00 a.m. We all had a very hard time sleeping; the kids couldn't sleep because of that cold place. After a while, everybody fell asleep.

I was so tired. I fell asleep and had a dream; I still remember it. I was walking in the river in my bare feet. As long as I was walking, the river got bigger and longer. I was so scared. I woke up and looked at my feet. I was all wet; it was almost like a river beside my bed because the ceiling was leaking badly. So, I woke up my friend Naza; she was asleep beside me on the floor with her kids. And then we woke up Nian, my other friend, and her kids. All our beds were wet, so we didn't sleep much that night. We all went to the other room to sleep with our men. Their room was very cold, but dry. Our room was warmer but wet, so neither room was good to sleep in, but we didn't have a choice.

The next day was a little sunny. After we had a breakfast, we got ready again to leave the house and go to the same place. We took everything with us, like our luggage and food for the kids. Ali told us if we didn't pass again, we could come back to his house. He would fix the room for us, and we could stay there until we leave. He was such a nice, decent man with a very generous heart.

When we got there, my husband, Shwan, tried to call the manager of the GDC over and over. Finally, after many tries, he reached the manager Mathew Lawson. Shwan asked him why we couldn't cross the border and leave the country like the rest of the people. He said he had no idea! He didn't know why! and said that we should be able to leave. He really didn't understand why not. He was surprised just like us!

After a long conversation with him, he told my husband to wait until he called back in three days to see what happened. One more time we went back to Ali's house. On away back to his house We bought some pillows, few blankets and more food. By the time we get back to the house, Ali had fixed the ceiling and put a nice rug on the floor for both rooms. Also, he brought a good-sized heater and more stuff for the kitchen.

After three days shwan and his friends went to the office at the checkpoint to call Mathew one more time, to know the answer from him, and know what he had to say either to let us cross the border or go back to our country. We were worried more than ever.

All of the ladies and kids stayed at home waiting with all our anger and sadness waiting to hear a good news, that would give us release, of our tough time we went through in the past days.

Two hours later they came back. It was not good news. The GDC manager told Shwan, "to wait two more weeks. If he couldn't do anything, he promised that he will help us find a different way to take us out of Kurdistan".

We stayed in that place two weeks, but we didn't get any answers. We spent all our money over the rent and food. We got sick. our kids got bord. We had a lot of stress. There were too many people in one small house, and there was a pregnant lady with six kids, so we decided to go back to our city and face our fate. Our hope disappeared for no reason. It was so unfair; no one recognized why this happen to us. It was just a deep dark secret for somebody. I believed one day we will know.

After two weeks Nian was so ready to deliver her baby. We were so terrified. If it happened in that dirty, cold house, what would we do? So, we all decided to leave the next morning. Each family got a different taxicab. We didn't want to go back to our city all together for safety purposes

Chapter 14

We went home. None of our family had any idea that we were still here and heading back home! Everyone went to their parents' houses. We did the same. It was a huge surprise for my family. I knocked on the door. It was 5:00 p.m. My sister opened the door! She was shocked to see me standing there. She didn't say a word. I said, "We didn't go; they didn't let us go." My voice was shaking, and tears were running down my cheeks like rain. I couldn't talk or do anything, but my sister hugged me.

She started crying and said, "It's OK, it's OK. Come in, hurry before anybody sees you. Get inside."

The kids were really confused. My daughter, Lana, didn't know exactly what was going on. She was so happy that we were going to the United States after her sadness of being away from her cousins and grandparents. Then she almost accepted being away from them; she had been ready to accept a new life in the United States with many new, exciting things that would happen when we get there. Suddenly nothing—we came back. She thought she was ready to make a new friend, and she thought it would be fun to start a new life. My son, Alan, didn't understand anything; he was too young, but he was crying most of the time.

Everyone was surprised and speechless. They were sad for us because we had already lost everything we own, and now our lives were in danger. My parents were happy to see us again, but they didn't want that to happen. My dad said, "I told you before, if anything went wrong, you are both welcome here, until you find another way to get out of the country. Here is not safe anymore for you."

My dad was really worried about what would happen.

Anyway, we stayed at my parents' house for two weeks. We couldn't go out. We had to hide ourselves from everyone, because we didn't know who we could trust. Shwan said, "I can't stay at home all the time." Before, he would spend most of his days working. But now he had to stay out of site. That was the most difficult thing for him to do. One of us was always working to making our own money; we never depended on anyone. It was very hard for us to be unemployed. We expended all our money in Zaxo. We were almost destitute and didn't like to borrow money from anyone.

These days passed like a nightmare. We were very angry; we didn't know what to do next. We knew we couldn't stay hiding forever, but we were scared. Shwan started looking for legal travel documents. At that time, people were forging passports for a large sum of money. It was hard to know the difference between the bogus and the real deal. Shwan wanted to buy a real one, even though it was very expensive. We wanted to go out through Turkey legally.

Fortunately, I still had some of my gold. Shwan's family offered help to us. I told him not to worry about money right now;

I would sell my gold. We would see if that gave us enough for the passports. First, he refused; he wanted me to keep my gold for myself, but in our culture, we believe in 'white money for a dark day.' Right now, we needed money, not jewelry.

I went with my mom to the jeweler that we had known for a long time. He bought my gold for a reasonable amount. I gave Shwan 6,000 DINAR to buy passports for all of us. At that time that was equivalent to about $20,000 for 4 legal passports. One more time we started to get ready. The passports were completed very quickly, in only three weeks. Everything was legal, everything was perfect, and we still had some money left. We had a very safe plan. We were going to Turkey. While there, we would go to the UN Refugee Agency (UNHCR), to make a VISA for us to go either to Europe or USA.

Shwan's family said they would help us as soon we arrive in Turkey. Most of them were already living in Europe. So far, so good. We decided to leave one week after we got the passports. This time, my mom wasn't happy at all, but we had to leave. We felt we did not belong in our country anymore. Sometimes when something hurts this much, you just have to keep it suppressed. There are no words that can describe our sorrow.

Everyone was sad and quiet that day. No one wanted to say goodbye, but my dad was always positive and always said, "Don't be mad, or even sad. When things go wrong, maybe God has a better plan for you." I knew my dad was right, but the situation was very tough. We were not criminals to run away. Shwan had worked with an American organization to support our family. That was our only crime. Saddam always looked for an excuse to hurt Kurds; it didn't matter how big or small the purpose.

The day we left, Shwan paid extra money to the driver to take us safely to Ibrahim xalil, the border between Kurdistan and Turky. He said, he would do his best.

Later that day, we got to Ibrahim xalil. It was eight hours straight. We were happy that we arrived, and we didn't have any problems.

The day was eighteen of February 1996 the time was 3: p.m. We got there, the place wasn't a big building, just simple office with some officer and employee. First Shwan went inside; after fifteen minuets, then they called me with Lana and Alan. They checked everything we had, even the kids, and they asked for the passports. Shwan had them all and gave them to a guy who looked like an officer. He took the passports and opened them page by page. Then he asked Shwan if it was his passport. Shwan said, "Sure, it's mine." With a big surprise tone voice. And then he looked at me and asked my name and some questions. I answered him.

Later he asked about our birthdates and many unnecessary questions; we answered everything right. After a long conversation with his associates around him (in the Turkish language; we didn't understand anything), he looked at us and said, "You are impostors. This passport is not real. You must leave this area right now, or I will call security to take you all to the jail." surprisingly. We looked at the officer and looked at each other. First, we didn't know what he was talking about. We looked at him. He said, "Hurry, hurry, get out!" We were still quiet and looked at each other. We were in shock again. We didn't believe what we heard. He was repeating himself many times, that we were not real, we were fake, and the names were not real. We still did not understand what he was talking about. I looked at Shwan. I said, "Did you understand what he just said?" He said, "No! I don't!"

And then Shwan asked the officer, (speaking in English language) "I really don't know why you are yelling at us, and why you are asking us to leave; what have we done wrong? Can you explain more to us? Please."

The officer looked at Shwan with a silly face and said, "Really, you don't know?" Shwan answered him in a very strong, angry voice, and said, "Really, we don't know, but I would like to know." The officer said, "Look, let me tell you this. About a month ago These names have crossed this border to Turkey; these names have already gone through this border, so how are you possibly telling me it's your name and your family's name? It can't be an accident. I can only believe that the real people have already passed. Now you're fake. So, you must leave this building right now." He took our passport and punched a hole in it. After I saw what he did, I got shocked. I couldn't walk, my legs got frozen with the terrible news.

Shwan was laughing and crying at the same time. I was crying, too, I feel like the room was spinning around and pass out. I don't know for how long but when I opened my eyes I saw myself laying on the flour. My kids were crying, shwan was crying and holding my hand. I remember he was saying, "please don't cry we are a life, we will find out who dos this to us. We will do this together. I promise you I will do everything to keep you all safe. I will never ever give up." That minute was the tougher time in my life. That was second time, and was all our hope, we spend everything we had. And again, we are not allowed to pass; because somebody used our Identifications and past.! That minute to me was like the end of the world I couldn't stop my tears. It was too much. We know the cheat was from our people, but we didn't know who it was. I asked him, "Now what? What should we do? Please let me talk to them. This is not right; we can't just go back to our city like that. We are in danger. They don't know. Let me tell them; maybe they can help us." Shwan didn't let me go talk to them" he says, "don't even try because simply They don't care about us. They are another enemy of Kurds, so let's go back home, we will find out."

We were tired of our lives. The kids started understanding that we feared the dictator Saddam, and now the Turks were threatening us too. So, sadly we left that horrible building and went to Zaxo to find a hotel to stay in that night, and we did.

Chapter 15

The next day, we went back home with all our disappointment, one more time. we took back with us another surprise for my family another sad story. The whole time on the way back home, I was thinking about my parents. How could I tell them what happened? And how would they react? It wasn't easy for them or for us. Going back home like this was more dangerous for us. That eight hours was too long.

When we were in the car, Shwan and I decided that we were not staying in my parents' house, but we had to rent a house until we knew what we do. We didn't have any backup plan because everything we did was 100 percent legal. After a long way, we got to my parents' house. I tried to smile and not show them how sad and mad I was. I wanted to make my dad happy by telling him that I knew my God had a better plan for us. That was why we couldn't go these times. Maybe the time was not ready yet for us. My mom opened the door. She was so surprised; she screamed very loud. I still remember that day. My mom passed out; she knew what had happened again. Shwan and I tried to take her inside the house. We looked for my dad; nobody was there.

After a little bit, my mom came to. She was looking at me and my kids and asking why we were there in her house. She wasn't sure if she was awake or dreaming, but Shwan told her, "No, you're not dreaming, Mom. We are here again in your house; we couldn't make it again this time." She started crying and hugging me very tightly. I tried to be strong; not cry with my mom, I said mom please don't do this, we are fine I'm sure what happened it's for our benefit, I believe if something meant to happen to us it will happen. We are not hiding ourselves anymore. I asked her about my dad. She said he was not home. He was at the doctor's office with my brother. Then we said we were not going to stay here, because my dad already wasn't feeling good. We didn't want to make it worse for him. My mom wanted us to stay, but we left.

We went to Shwan's brother's house. I told my mom not to tell my dad about us until he felt better. After two days, we started looking for a small house to rent for our family we want to stay and watch maybe things going better for us at least for a while. Of course, we spend our money, what left was just a little. again, I must seal the rest of my gold. this time I sold even my wedding ring and my daughter's earring, and her necklace, just to have money in our hands.

One more time, we got hurt from the unknown. But it didn't matter who was it; in the end, we were homeless. We didn't have home, money, job neither safety. Our family always helped us, but they couldn't give us our safety.

We made their lives more dangerous and miserable than ever, because our situation.

Chapter 16

That period of our life was very hard. Shwan and I decided to open a temporary simple home for our small family. One of my brother's friends had a small house he wanted to give to us just for a few months to stay in.

We really appreciated his help, but we decided to give him some money when we got help from Shwan's family in Europe. We got that house. My sister, brother, and the rest of my family brought us some things for the kitchen, like a small stove and dishes. They also brought carpet and a small rug, with some foam to use as a bed, and pillows and lots of blankets. The house was only one bedroom, with one living room and a small kitchen. Because we didn't have furniture, I only used the kitchen for everything. We didn't have a counter or China cabinet to put in a plate, and silverware anymore.

We didn't have a refrigerator or television or a sofa and chair to sit on. We didn't have anything that belonged to us, not even our lives! We spend our life day by day. In the beginning, our new, strange live was very difficult.

We were facing many problems. We couldn't look for a job; we needed money but couldn't make money. We also were not used to borrowing money from anyone, not even my dad. We never depended on anyone. Every day, our life got more complicated than ever.

The weather was very bad that winter. We barely could buy kerosene for our heater to keep the house warm; it was working with kerosene. We had to buy food for our kids. I never lived poor in my whole life. But I tasted how you feel when you are hungry, but you don't have a piece of bread in your house. Or you must hide food from your kids, even if you know they are hungry, because we couldn't afford three meals. I know how it feels when you had all family and friends around you, but after you are poor, some of them doesn't cares or even comes to visit to see if you need anything.

People can change a lot.

Shwan never stopped looking for a way to get out safely.

This time, he decided to go by himself with a group of people. The kids and I stayed home. I didn't agree, because I knew how bad that way was to go through Iran. He made his own decision that he was leaving the next week because they told him the way they will taking; it would be clear with no problems at all. He was so excited, but I was so worried. The next week came fast, and he left one early morning. The kids were still asleep; he kissed them and kissed me. Our plans were that he would go alone with a group. When he got there, he would meet his old friend in Iran. Then he would go to Europe to meet his family and then he would make a case for us. Then he would come back and take us there. It was a long process, but that was the only way we could get away from the danger.

That day, I was so sad, especially when Alan woke up, he was looking around himself like he lost something in the house. I knew he was looking for his father because he never acts like that before. He always sees his daddy's home especially after we came back from Zaxo. the first time, Lana and Alan become very close to their daddy, later Alan knows he's not home, he start crying; I told him, "your daddy will be back. he went to buy food." I was preparing the breakfast for myself, I don't know why suddenly I felt hangry I wanted to eat, Alan was crying I was lying to him to make him stop crying, but Lana knew where her daddy went; that is why she was sitting in the corner of that kitchen. She put her head down inside her knees and cried very quietly. I requested her to stop crying and help me to keep Alan busy because I wasn't feel good and I wanted her to come eat breakfast, but she told me, "No, I'm waiting on my daddy. You told Alan my dad went to buy food, so he will be back soon, right?" I begged her to stop that and come eat her food, but again she refused. She said, "I don't want my dad to go alone. Why are we not going with him? I miss my daddy. If we die, let's die together." I was so shocked when I heard that from a seven-year-old. I couldn't hold my terries longer; Then I started cry. I went to hold Alan and hug Lana; Suddenly I felt a pain in my stomach and felt very sick. I had to run to the bathroom. I threw up, and I felt very cold. I came back to the kitchen. I tried to drink some hot tea and lay down, but I felt very dizzy. The room was spinning in front of my eyes. Lana asked me, "Mommy, are you OK?" I said, "Yes, baby." She said, "No, you look very sick, Mommy. I'm afraid."

I was very sick. I threw up three times until noon, but I didn't have anyone close to me to leave the kids with to go to the doctor's office. Later that day my sister came to see me. I was so happy when she came. As soon she got to my house, I went to the doctor. I told her to sit until I came back. I already told her that I was not feeling good. The doctor checked everything, for maybe ten minutes; then she sent me to do blood work and other tests. I waited in her office until she gave me the results. It was almost 7:00 p.m. when she called me inside her office. She said with a big smile that I' m pregnant! And the baby is eight weeks. That was the last thing I wanted to hear, just because the time wasn't right; our financial situation was very bad, and our life was so hard and difficult. My first reaction to the doctor was crying. She looked at me, very spuriously, she asked why I'm crying. I told her this is not a right time to having a baby, I told her about my life. She said, "So? Maybe this baby brings you happiness. Maybe your life is going to get better. Who knows? Always be thankful for what you have, and you are still young. You and your husband can make a lot of changes in your life. There are a lot of opportunities. Keep the baby and be happy. God will help you." I was about to ask her to do an abortion, but after what she said, I stopped talking and I left. It was so sudden. *Oh, God, why this is happening to me now?* But I tried to think about what the doctor told me: "Maybe this baby would bring you happiness and good luck!" I was so confused. I hated thinking about abortion. How could I have another baby? I can't have a baby right now; this was not the time. This baby makes our leaving process impossible.

I had many bad thoughts, I stopped in the second. Another thought was maybe it's a good thing happening for us. I got home, when I went inside, I knew my sister was still there with my kids.

I heard her voice she was loudly talking and laughing. The kids were happy too. I opened the kitchen door. I went inside. I saw Shwan was there! I said, "Oh my God!" and I got so happy. When I saw him, I thought all my bad thoughts and all my problems had vanished. He looked so tired and dirty; all his clothes were muddy. I jumped to hug him, and the kids were very happy too. He looked at me and said, "Have you been crying?" I said no. He said, "Yes, I see your eyes are red, but tell me why you went to visit a doctor, what is wrong?"

I said, "I'm doing good; I have just some colds." My sister was watching me very carefully; she came closer to me and said, "By the way, what did the doctor say to you? Are you pregnant? Do you have a baby?" She was saying that with a big smile. I was so surprised. How did she know? I said I don't know!

Shwan said, "How do you not know?" I said, "Yes, I know. They both looked at me and waited for me to say something, but I asked him a question to change the subject I said, "You tell me how you came back and what happened to you!" He said oh the guide wasn't sharp enough, so we missed the road and then we found our self among pasdaran the Iranian military, so they open fire on us, then we had to leave the area, and I decide to come back. But later he told me the reason was he missed us. He thought that plan was too long to be together again and too dangerous to go to Europe, so he decided to come back.

My sister left. We had been happy that night because he came back, but I was worried about how to tell him. I was sure he would be angry, especially with the baby eight weeks. It was hard to do anything, and I didn't want to miscarriage my baby.

The next morning, I woke up with the same pain and was throwing up. Shwan woke up too. He came after me, looked at me, and said, "What is going on, woman?" I said, "Nothing, it's my stomach." He said, "Are you sure it's nothing?" I said no and I went back to bed, but I couldn't sleep again. He said, "Don't lie or hide. Are you pregnant?" I said, "Yes, I am. What do you want me to do? Don't ask me to do an abortion; I will not do that."

He said, "Wait, wait. When did you figure it out?" I said, "Yesterday. The doctor told me the baby is eight weeks, I'm not doing anything to my baby."

He sat on his bed and looked at me. He said, "You're crazy. Do you know what this means?"

I said, "Yes, but maybe this baby brings us good luck. Why not? I'm concerned, but I will keep this baby." He didn't respond to anything, but he starts playing with Alan and Lana, I tried to keep myself warm because I had a lot of stomach pain and nauseous, then he looked at me he said, "I'm going out would you like anything to eat"?

I said, "no but I want you make me a hot tea I'm very cold" he made me a mint tea, he sat dawn beside me he said, are you sure you want to keep this baby?

I said yes, with my very strong voice,

He said, "do you realized this baby possibly destroy our plan"?

I said, "no its not; maybe this baby makes our plan easier, maybe this baby it's a gift, maybe this baby our guide, God send to showing us our path, who knows"? then he looked at me without saying anything and he left.

Around noon, he came back with many bags of vegetables, meat and chicken, and some fruit. I said, "Why did you buy all this food? We need to save our money. Since you came back, your family will not send the help you wanted." He said, "Yes, they did.

I have money, and since we have a pregnant lady here, we have to have healthy food for her."

I said, "Are you sure?"

He said yes.

I said, "You are not angry?"

He said, "Yes, I am, but what can I do? It's our baby. We should love him and take care of you." I was very happy. It was like the big, heavy weight on my shoulder had disappeared.

Last chapter

After one week, my neighbor knocked on the door. She said someone on the phone wanted to talk to Shwan (we didn't have a phone, but my neighbor did). Shwan run very quickly. After five minutes, he came back with a very happy face. He jumped and hugged me. I said, "What is this? Who was on the phone?" He said, "My cousin. He has a very good way to help us out. It's 100 percent safe!" I asked how and where. We tried three ways that did not happen. What was left that we hadn't tried? He said we would go to Syria to the United Nations High Commissioner for Refugees (UNHCR) in Damascus. We would give them our case; they would accept, and after three months, we would transfer to the United States. He told me it's the only way that was guaranteed. I wanted to believe him, but I couldn't. I was so worried because I couldn't take any more surprises. We'd all had enough.

That day we were happy and scared. We were thinking and planning what to do next. We had to be very careful; this was the last chance. Soon he started calling his friends in Syria, and his family in Europe to make sure that everything would be on time with no more surprises. He decided to leave in one week at least. But I, and kids remain in our city, until he goes to UNHCR in Damascus. If they accepted him, he would call me to go there. Then we all would wait there until they made paperwork for us to go to the United States. We didn't know how long it's taken but we planned everything right. He left again. I stayed with Lana and Alan.

After three days shwan called me, he told me he rent a small house with two guys, they leaving the house soon and he told me he went to the UNHCR and he already had an interview with the person who has a higher position. And he made a big case for us. His cousin prepared a legal paper that help us to stay in Syria. (His cousin was working as a lawyer.)

My mom was coming from time to time to stay with us. Sometimes my sister with her kids and sometimes my brother with his family would come. We all would eat and sleep in that small kitchen. with all my worries I was happy because; once again I'm surrounded by my lovely caring family who always make a smile on my face, and they were always around me. My life was very simple but had meaning.

I was waiting every day on a phone call from Shwan to tell me good news. But nothing. I was so busy with the kids. They were asking for their daddy, but I had to explain everything for them. They didn't understand much.

I wasn't feeling good most of the time because of my pregnancy. My doctor thought all my difficulties in pregnancy came from my stressful live I had a past few month. I was living in the sudden, stress, shock, and worry most of the time. Every time I went for a checkup with my doctor, she always Asking me to try hard not thinking about past but think about my new baby that coming soon and he need a healthy mother. I was trying very hard, but I had too much stress still.

Shwan sent me a long fax one day explaining everything, that he did another interview with one of the very important people from UNHCR. He was American. Shwan said, "When I told him about our story, he was really upset, and he promised that he will help us and work on our case seriously." Shwan was very happy about his interview. That day I took a very deep breath after a long time, and I thanked God for everything.

He told me I had to be there for our next interview, because they needed to see me there with my kids. Soon they asked for me He would let me know a week before. That time, I wasn't worried about anything anymore, just us, my kids, and me. No house, no car, no furniture. We had been waiting and waiting—nothing. Seven months passed, but we were waiting. I had one more week to deliver my baby. I got a call from Shwan telling me I had to be there next week. I said, "OK, I'm trying to get ready even before the time," but the next day, around evening I felt I had some pain in my back, but I said, to myself it's just normal pain I ignored it. After few hours the pain increased. I had to call my sister. She came with my sister in-law, and then my neighbor she came. The pain got worse and worse. The time was getting late My sister said, "Let's go to the hospital." I didn't want to because I still had one more week to deliver the baby. I thought it was just the normal beginning pain. I was thinking, *what if Shwan calls again for something important?* I didn't want to go to the hospital. My sister in-law, she was a nurse she said, "this pain means your baby is very close, we need to go to the hospital" but I waited one more hour, I couldn't handle the pain, so we all went to the hospital the time was 10:pm very cold night it was snowing and dark everywhere the power was off too. Before we leave, I asked my neighbor if she could stay with my kids until we are coming home, with all my pain I know that I'm not staying long in the hospital, she was a very sweet lady; I loved her so much. So, she babysits my kids that night, after nine hours, I had my lovely baby boy Ary. He was so hairy but very cute. Later we all went home to my parents' house. My mom and my sister made a nice bed for me and the baby, that morning my mom she cooked a lot of different food, our traditional is when we have a baby the mother must make halwa, it's a sweet dessert for the lady to who has deliver baby to eat to increase a pain. At the same night Shwan called but my neighbor told him we were in the hospital, and we had a baby boy. She said, he was so happy: "He wants you to be ready next week. He will call you back again before the time."

Time went fast. I was surrounded with my family. They took very good care of me and my kids. Everyone was busy with us. My dad was so happy for us. I stayed at my parent house until we left, I never went back to my house. Two weeks past my sisters went to clean that house and give the key back to that nice, wonderful man who help my family for long time more than nine_ month. My sister she brings all our clothes we had and my kids' stuff to take with us; we didn't have many things. I was so ready to leave. My kids they missed their daddy. I got a last phone call from Shwan telling me that he would wait on the border tomorrow. He told me to bring food for the kids because maybe we stay long hours on the border. (That border is between Kurdistan and Syria its called feshxapoor.)

Everything went fast. The next day at 5:00 a.m., my brother in-law came with a taxicab, and we left my parents' house for the third times. This time, everyone was smiling and looking happy for us. After seven hours we got to the border. The first minute we got out from the taxi, Alan saw his dad between all that crowd. There was a river between us, but it was not too deep, not too wide, but we had to use the boat to cross that river. He was waiting on us, but Alan called him many times: "Daddy, Daddy, I miss you, Daddy!" before He wasn't talking much, but after he saw his dad, he couldn't stop talking. We got across that river, and there was a bus waiting for us. We got inside that small old bus until we got to Qamishli after a few hours. Then we took some rest. Then we went to another big bus to take us to Damascus. After nine hours, we got there. It was 7:00 a.m. the next day. No one slept all the time on that bus. We were so happy; we didn't believe we got out of the danger. We went to the house that Shwan was living in with the other people for a few days at the area called masakn barza. Then we went to another house with a couple of families.

Later, after two days, we went to UNHCR together to a final interview with the manager of the whole office he was American. Everyone came to meet us and know us. They wanted to help our family. They were honest. They felt so sorry for what happened to us, but it was still a mystery for everyone who knew about our story. After our meeting with more than one person. After almost five months, one early Saturday morning the director of the UNHCR called Shwan. He said, "Your family's visas are ready, and your tickets are ready as well." To America! That news was the best news ever. Quickly Shwan went to the office to get all our visas and tickets. When he came home, we start to prepare ourselves ready. The next day, we flew from Damascus international airport to Frankfort international airport in Germany and

the next day we landed at the Chicago airport on March 10, 2000. At 2:00 pm
   Welcome to America.

To be continued...

Ingram Content Group UK Ltd.
Milton Keynes UK
UKHW040629290623
424267UK00004B/157